THE WEST HIGHLAND WAY

Fort William

Kinloch

Loch Leven

Loch Etive

Tyndrum

Loch Lom

Firth of Clyde

THE WEST HIGHLAND WAY

n

idge of Orchy

Crianlarich

Aberfoyle

Drymen

Milngavie

Glasgow   Edinburgh

Dundee

The West Highland Way

ABOUT THE AUTHOR

A writer and photographer since 1978, Terry Marsh specialises in the outdoors, the countryside, walking and travel worldwide. He is the author of 45+ books including the award-winning Cicerone guides to the *Coast to Coast Walk* and the *Shropshire Way*, along with guides to the *Pennine Way*, the *Dales Way* and the *Severn Way*.

Terry is a Fellow of the Royal Geographical Society (FRGS) and of the Society of Antiquaries of Scotland (FSA Scot), and a Member of the Society of Authors, MENSA, the NUJ and the Outdoor Writers' Guild. He is a regular contributor to *Living France*, *Cumbria*, *Dalesman* and *Quicksilver*, and an occasional contributor to *In Britain*. Terry lectures on 'Writing about Travel' and 'The Creative Skills of Travel Writing' at Burton Manor College, Wirral, Cheshire.

Widely travelled, Terry's main areas of interest are England, Scotland, Wales, France, the Isle of Man and Australia.

THE WEST HIGHLAND WAY

by
Terry Marsh

2 POLICE SQUARE, MILNTHORPE, CUMBRIA LA7 7PY
www.cicerone.co.uk

Second edition 2003
Reprinted 2005, 2007, 2009, 2010
ISBN-13: 978 1 85284 369 4
ISBN-10: 1 85284 369 1
© Terry Marsh 1997, 2003

First edition 1997

Printed by MCC Graphics, Spain

A catalogue record for this book is available from the British Library.
All photographs are by the author unless otherwise stated.

ACKNOWLEDGEMENTS

The process of writing a book such as this is inordinately more complex (I hope) than the act of following the walk. It is a task made considerably easier by an increasingly rare breed of individual who actually doesn't mind helping people along, by the simple expedient of companionship along the way, by providing free accommodation, transport and information, and by the occasional string-pulling that enables a hard-pressed writer to keep to deadlines and produce a sound and coherent end product.

In this context I have to thank Virgin Trains and what was then CrossCountry Trains Limited for travel to and from Scotland, a facility I found immensely useful; the Scottish Youth Hostels Association for accommodation at Rowardennan, Crianlarich and Glen Nevis; everyone at the Argyll, the Isles, Loch Lomond, Stirling and Trossachs Tourist Board for arranging accommodation; Donald Powell, also of the Argyll, the Isles, Loch Lomond, Stirling and Trossachs Tourist Board for permission to use folkloric tales from documents published under the auspices of the tourist board; John Campbell of Crianlarich for fascinating extracts of folklore and local history; Ron and Tom for their company, always appreciated, between Crianlarich and Fort William during the first run, and, last but not least, my son Martin who accompanied me during the whole of the second visit.

Front cover: Crossing Ba Bridge on the West Highland Way

CONTENTS

WEST HIGHLAND WAY ROUTE

Advice to Readers

Readers are advised that while every effort is taken by the author to ensure the accuracy of this guidebook, changes can occur which may affect the contents. It is advisable to check locally on transport, accommodation, shops, etc, but even rights of way can be altered. Paths can be affected by forestry work, landslip or changes of ownership.

The publisher would welcome notes of any such changes.

This book was originally compiled in accordance with the *Guidelines for the Writers of Path Guides* published by the Outdoor Writers' Guild.

INTRODUCTION TO THE FIRST EDITION (1997)

When Walt Unsworth rang me up to ask if I could shelve the eternally on-going encyclopaedia of the countryside I was working on for him and go off to do a guidebook to the West Highland Way, I confess I delayed my response by a good two nanoseconds, mainly because I didn't want to appear too eager. But, I thought, if I don't do it, Walt will only get someone else to sort it out, so why not? I agreed, reluctantly. Well, it isn't every day you get a publisher throwing work your way – usually you have to grovel a bit first!

The truth is, I had driven up and down the Loch Lomond, Rannoch and Glencoe roads to Fort William for what seemed like an eternity, listening to the strains of Mike Oldfield and Rick Wakeman, and frequently glancing enviously across at serious-faced West Highland Wayfarers trudging through the rain in Glencoe, or cowering beneath heavy packs north of Tyndrum, and I felt that I wanted to share the same evidently transcendental experience. So when the chance came in the form of a money-making method, I leapt at it – after that two nanoseconds' delay, of course.

With untypical aplomb I rummaged about in search of my backpacking sack, the Trangias and numerous non-essential accessories I always take when backpacking, and then set about the tea bag and biscuit logistics, planning to complete the trek at the end of October 1995, scoot back to base and type it up speedily for publication in the spring of 1996. Sadly, I overlooked the fact that during the time I was there the whole country reverts from daft time to GMT, which left me with an inordinately long walk from Inveroran to Kinlochleven to do in one day, the last three hours of which were going to be in darkness. Not a problem in normal circumstances, but I was supposed to be working, and I couldn't write about what I couldn't see. So, at the Little Chef in Tyndrum, while consulting a Cajun chicken and chips, Plan B was devised, namely, go home and finish the walk in the spring. As a result, the poor souls at Crianlarich youth hostel who thought they had seen the last of me had to put up with me again, but they were quite brave about it.

More to the point, I got to see the Way in two seasons, and felt I had gained by doing so. In October, the temperatures had been ideal for backpacking, and the light even better for photography. By May, most of the snow had cleared from the mountains, the rivers and burns were manageable, and the light just as splendid.

I shall, unquestionably, go back and do it again, without the monetary incentive, just for the pleasure. I have never enjoyed doing a trail guide quite so much.

Approaching its twentieth year, the West Highland Way was the first officially designated long-distance route in Scotland, established under the Countryside (Scotland) Act, 1967. It runs, officially, for 152km (95 miles) from the outskirts of Glasgow to Fort William, and in the process contrives to experience an enormously wide variety of landscapes and walking conditions. It is neither easy nor outrageously demanding, though inclement weather can certainly raise the stakes a few notches, and it is not the most ideal route on which to set about one's first experience of long distance walking.

There is, too, a great association between much of the Way and the historical past of Scotland. It crosses three major areas of great significance in Scottish history from the lands of Lennox, through Breadalbane and on to Lochaber. Much of the route pursues ancient drove roads or old military roads built to help in the control of Jacobite clansmen, and the study of these aspects alone is a fascinating and worthwhile preoccupation.

The idea for the Way is not as recent as might be supposed. It originates as long ago as the 1930s and 1940s, but it was in the aftermath of the Pennine Way success story that embryonic notions began to develop to maturity. Approval for the Way to be officially developed was given in September 1974, and the route opened on 6 October 1980 by Lord Mansfield, Minister of State at the Scottish Office.

Because it does make use of those old drove roads and military roads, which in turn have been fairly faithfully followed by twentieth-century roads and railway links, the resulting route is never far from help, though it can seem it on a bad day. Only as you cross Rannoch Moor and pass through the Lairig Mor beyond Kinlochleven do you acquire any real sense of isolation. Yet the Way's proximity to such modern trappings of civilisation rarely impinges on the pleasure you gain from the walk. Yes, there are moments when you can hear the traffic and come perilously close to it, and yes, there are times when the traffic seems always in view, somewhere. But you must set that against a walk of great quality and distinction, that passes through a landscape second to none. Often all it takes to shun these 'problems' is a convenient boulder or sheltered hollow, and you could be a million miles from anywhere.

For me, the great pleasure of the Way derives from the many changes in its character, as it moves through different geological zones, from lowland Scotland to the highlands, from the pastoral introduction as you move northwards from Milngavie, to the loveliness that is Loch Lomond. Beyond that you enter the realms of Glen Falloch and Strath Fillan, glens flanked by great mountains that were once cloaked by the mantle of an ancient Caledonian pine forest.

North of Tyndrum the Way sets

Ascending from Bridge of Orchy to Man Carraigh

about tackling Rannoch Moor, largely on routes formerly used by drovers. As a result it is well trodden and never in doubt. But it is along this section that you find yourself more remote from outside help than at any other time along the walk. On a good day the walking is a delight, but, in spite of the comparative ease of the conditions underfoot, poor weather can soon turn delight to disaster. Anyone not bound for the oasis that is the King's House Hotel should think twice, if the weather is especially changeable, before leaving the security of the Bridge of Orchy or Inveroran.

Touching only briefly on Glencoe, the Way presses on from Kingshouse, heading for Kinlochleven, the Lairig Mor and Fort William. I found the short stretch between Kingshouse and Altnafeadh, which is seldom far from the heavy and speeding traffic on the A82, to be the least appealing section of the whole walk. As you approach Altnafeadh you stride along within feet of the traffic, and in wet conditions are sure to get a good drenching from spray. To avoid the danger there is an alternative line that follows the River Coupall, with much to be said in its favour, though it gives a much lower view of the glen than the main route.

Between Altnafeadh and the end of the Way at Fort William the quality of the walking remains high. Forestry plantations cloak the hills on the south side of Glen Nevis, but they are rarely oppressive. Before that, the long, winding approach to Kinlochleven and the ensuing flight across the southern flanks of the Mamores through Lairig Mor is excellent walking, and a fitting final stage for an outstanding walk.

INTRODUCTION TO THE
SECOND EDITION (2003)

Inevitably the time came when it was prudent to look at revising this guide, so the route was walked in its entirety in May 2002: it rained every day!

Remarkably, very little had changed – certainly nothing of the route was different. A larger number of B&Bs along the way were cashing in on its success story – nothing wrong with that of course – and the pack carrying service, which only the stoical will ignore, had come into its own. Not all long-distance walks lend themselves to a pack carrying service, but this is one that does.

What really stood out was the tremendous sense of camaraderie that developed among walkers travelling on the same day. Over a period of a week, while you're not travelling in one another's pockets, you do keep meeting the same people and share experiences. That's good; that's as it should be. Get out of sync, and suddenly you don't know anyone.

Around 17,000 people complete the West Highland Way each year. That's not bad by any standards. Far more set off and don't finish; some don't even complete the first day. The impression I gained is that too many of those who think they can do the Way are ill prepared, have little experience of day-long walking, day after day, and have equipment that is anything but tried and tested.

In this revised edition I have stripped out the artificial route 'sections' I had imposed on the first edition. In reality these are not needed. The danger is that this creates an artificial target, which is wholly irrelevant. Each day's walking should be within your own capability. Use taxis to shunt you about if necessary, but do not attempt to do more than you can comfortably manage. And be prepared to modify your plans.

EXPLANATORY NOTES

DISTANCES AND ASCENT

To ensure accuracy when giving distances and ascent, detailed measurements were originally made using OS Outdoor Leisure Maps, at a scale of 1:25,000, where necessary measuring distances at 100-metre intervals, and calculating vertical heights to within five metres. There is inevitably a lack of precision in this, and my measurement of distances may differ slightly from the official distances; any such discrepancy, however, is unlikely to be significant.

USING THE GUIDE

The guide is divided into explanatory notes, advice on how to go about planning the walk and about walking it, a description of the route, an accommodation guide, some useful addresses and finally a reading list. The latter is a list of what I regard as essential and supplementary reading, some or all of which will enhance your experience of the walk. The accommodation listing can never be complete since the West Highland Way is a developing tourist industry of its own, and changes occur each year which instantly make my list out of date. If you find somewhere that is good, and not listed by me, please drop me a line via the publisher so that I can include the address in any revision of the guide.

In the text the route description is given in normal type. Author's comments, observations and general background information are indented in the main body of the text and in the sidebar.

Although the route description is written in four sections, no attempt has been made to construct 'day length' sections – that is for you, but please be sure not to overstretch yourself. The West Highland Way is immensely pleasurable, but not when you are weary.

Keep it simple; keep it within your capability.

View of Loch Lomond from Conic Hill

Striding out along the old Glencoe road, Rannoch Moor

according to a plan I might suggest – the following table (below) includes suggestions only. I originally planned to do the walk in six days, which would be quite demanding and allow no rest (or easy) days. Seven or eight days would be much more comfortable if you have limited experience of distance walking.

You can make nine days of it by breaking the Drymen to Rowardennan section at Balmaha, allowing time to visit Inchcailloch, which illustrates the point that the walk must become what you want it to be. It is not a forced march, something you have to do in so many days (unless, of course, commitments mean that you do). The Way is a walk to be enjoyed leisurely; something to take your time over and to use as a gateway to exploration of the countryside that lies to either side of it.

Start	6 days	7 days	8 days
Milngavie	Drymen	Drymen	Drymen
Drymen	Rowardennan	Rowardennan	Rowardennan
Rowardennan	Crianlarich	Crianlarich	Inverarnan
Inverarnan			Crianlarich
Crianlarich	Inveroran	Bridge of Orchy	Bridge of Orchy
Bridge of Orchy		Kingshouse	Kingshouse
Kingshouse		Kinlochleven	Kinlochleven
Inveroran	Kinlochleven		
Kinlochleven	Fort William	Fort William	Fort William

ACCOMMODATION

For a walk that spends a deal of its time away from civilisation, the Way is well supported by accommodation throughout its entire length. But it is not over endowed, so don't take accommodation for granted; book ahead – a day at a time may suffice at quiet times of the year. In the main tourist season, however, there is pressure on all the accommodation along the Way, while in the quieter months some closes down altogether.

This guide contains an accommodation listing, but you should consult the appropriate tourist boards (see 'Useful Addresses') for information on the up-to-date situation, which is changing all the time.

The range of accommodation is quite remarkable. In addition to the B&Bs, guest houses, hotels, and camp sites that you would expect, the Way boasts three good youth hostels ideally placed for Wayfarers, plus a number of bothies, 'wigwam' shelters (basic wooden structures without facilities – though there are always facilities nearby), bunkhouses and private hostels. You will even find small, woodland camp sites set within the boundaries of the Loch Lomond Park, specifically created with walkers in mind.

TRANSPORT

With few exceptions, the West Highland Way is seldom far from a road or a railway, so it is feasible to do it in short sections using public transport. The services, however, are not frequent, so if you are thinking of trying this option, do ensure you have up-to-date timetables. You can get them at the information centres in Glasgow and Fort William, or at bus and rail stations.

One interesting possibility,

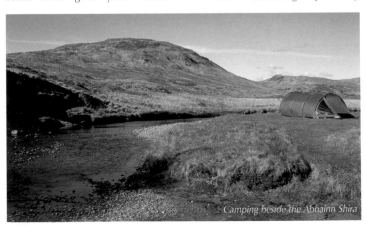

Camping beside the Abhainn Shira

Descending from Rannoch Moor into Glencoe

thought of but not tried, is to travel by car to roughly the half way point at Crianlarich. Leave the car there (obviously you will need to make some arrangement to garage it safely, but one of the hotels may well oblige, especially if you are planning to spend nights there), and then go by train from Crianlarich to Glasgow. Walk the Way, and catch the train back from Fort William to Crianlarich. One of the advantages of this is that you can leave a complete change of clothing, extra food supplies, maps, etc. in the car, changing over at the mid-way point.

EQUIPMENT

All walkers have their own preferences in the matter of equipment and clothing. When extending day walking into multiple day walking much the same general items are needed, with the emphasis on being able to stay warm and dry (as much as possible), and comfortable in all weather conditions.

The following list may be found a useful reminder – rucksack (comfortable, well padded, appropriate to backpacking rather than day walking, and preferably already used by you, if only on trial walks), boots, socks (and spare socks), trousers (or shorts, etc. but not shorts alone), underclothes, shirt, midwear (e.g. pullover) and spare, wind- waterproof jacket and overtrousers, hat, gloves, maps, compass, torch (with spare battery and bulbs), whistle, first aid kit, survival bag or space blanket, food and drink, insect repellent, ablution tackle, including half a roll of toilet tissue (for emergencies), small hand towel.

Campers will also need such additional weighty items as tent, sleeping bag, Karrimat, cooking equipment and utensils.

Pedal bin liners will be found to have a number of useful purposes: keeping wet clothes separate from dry in the sack, containing burst packets of food, cereal, etc. and rubbish, until a suitable disposal point can be reached, and for insulating dry socks from wet boots when walking.

Take a notebook and keep a personal record of your experiences, or a paperback book to read.

With few opportunities along the Way to obtain cash, it becomes vitally important that you estimate your money requirements in advance. There are banks in Milngavie and Drymen, but after that nothing until Kinlochleven and Fort William. A cheque book and banker's card can usually be used to obtain cash from post offices which, in addition to the places where there are banks, can be found in Ardlui, Crianlarich and Tyndrum.

PACK CARRYING SERVICES

The proximity of the West Highland Way to major highways has seen a new service evolve, that of pack carrying. A number of small companies and taxi firms offer to carry your heavy pack from one location to another on a daily or occasional basis. If you have difficulty carrying heavy loads, and would appreciate the benefits of doing the Way with a day sack, perhaps the pack carrying service is the thing to use. Details are included in 'Useful addresses'.

DOGS

There are many sections of the West Highland Way where because of farming concerns dogs are simply not permitted, not even on a lead. In view of this it would be folly to think of tackling the Way with a dog, however harsh it may seem for an outdoor dog to have to stay at home.

CYCLING

The West Highland Way makes use of many old roads, but it is a route designated for walkers. Many parts of the route are possible on suitable bikes, but as a whole it is not for cyclists.

Buachaille Etive Mor

WALKING THE WEST HIGHLAND WAY

Having now walked and written about quite a few long-distance walks, I was very pleased to see how sensitively and sensibly the West Highland Way has been waymarked. The emblem is simply a white thistle within a hexagon on a post, and with only three minor exceptions I have not found waymarks that were super-fluous. Where the line of the route is abundantly clear, as for example across Rannoch Moor, there is no waymarking at all, which is as it should be. Those responsible for waymarking should be commended.

Even with this unobtrusive level of waymarking, it is perfectly feasible to travel the route without real fear of getting lost, and you could argue that this guide does no more than put flesh on what would be the very bare bones of the waymarks. Hopefully, it does more than that, and provides a measure of reassurance and guidance to those who need it, and a modicum of background information for those who want to take in the landscape and the culture through which the Way passes.

WEATHER

Over the many years that I have been backpacking in Scotland I have at various times encountered weather that has grilled my ears to an acute degree of tenderness and at others drenched me so thoroughly that it would have been simpler, but infinitely more embarrassing, to walk with nothing on at all! Both extremes should be expected and catered for by anyone contemplating the West Highland Way. Only those who don't think in terms of such weather conditions are likely to find themselves facing uncomfortable and (at the extreme) potentially dangerous conditions.

Beinn Odhar

In Scotland, weather statistics are a meaningless exercise, made all the more pointless by the fact that many walkers on the West Highland Way simply cannot sit at home until the weather looks like settling for a week or so and then zoom to Glasgow to begin the walk. The reality is that you get whatever weather is on offer, and you, the walker, must be capable of coping with it. Someone once told me that there is no such thing as bad weather, just inadequate clothing. I know what he meant, but I have often said, usually of the Isle of Skye, that if you expect Cold, Wet and Windy, and prepare for it, then anything else is a bonus; approach the West Highland Way in the much the same frame of mind: expect the worst, and when you find beautiful days of perfect walking weather then you'll come to understand that the sun really does shine on the righteous – and, as I do, start looking round for him or her.

If you set your sights on May and June, September and October, the chances are you will get the best and most settled weather.

One of the least expected consequences of bad weather is the effect it can have on even the tiniest burns, turning them into raging torrents that can prove very difficult to cross. To a large extent this has been anticipated by the managing authorities for the Way, and footbridges installed wherever this is likely to occur, but there is always at least one exception that seems set on proving the rule. Unless time is genuinely of the essence, the wisest way of dealing with these extreme conditions is to retreat and sit them out in safety and comfort for a while. They seldom last long, and, with the possible exception of misty conditions, usually clear up in a brief period of time.

PESTS

One of the purgatorial experiences of walking in Scotland is the ubiquitous midge, a tiny stinging insect that

Glencoe from Kingshouse

Loch na h-achlaise and the Black Mount summits

in times gone by, including a paper mill and a cotton mill, so the connection is a plausible one.

Tramcars from Glasgow once swayed their way to Milngavie; now their place has been taken by a modern railway, and during the summer months there is a distinct impression that this is a charter service for Wayfarers.

The route begins with some (inconsequential) controversy about the exact start of the West Highland Way; immediately adjacent to the railway station is a large board announcing the start of the Way, while local opinion considers that the Way begins at a neat obelisk – unveiled by a local councillor on 20 November 1992 – in the centre of town. The distinction is immaterial since if you come by train you start from the station anyway, just as everyone did before the obelisk was built; if you come by any other means of public or private transport, you still have to walk to the obelisk, which stands in the middle of a neat pedestrianised oasis.

From the station go left and through an underpass to ascend steps into Station Road. Keep ahead through a pedestrian precinct, passing the Cross Keys Inn to reach the obelisk. Here, turn right (conspicuously way-marked), and down a ramped walkway to effect an ignominious start to the walk, through a supermarket service area. Cross the car park, trending right, and ignoring the tempting bridge on the left. Walk out to meet a road, turn left on a tarmac path beside a burn. The Way soon goes under a road, and enters a tree-lined and acoustically-screened cutting with steep, sloping banks, that once accommodated a small railway serving a paper mill on Allander Water.

Within minutes the sound of a modestly busy town is left well behind, as the trackbed shepherds you on to the rear of Milngavie Library and a leisure centre. Quite soon you leave the railway route, going left into woodland to reach a large pond. As you do, go right and right again a few strides later to court Allander Water through pleasant woodland, a brief riparian ramble in the company of dippers and grey wagtails.

Ignore the bridge that spans Allander Water, and

press on beside the burn into the more open expanse of Allander Park. These early stages of the walk are inevitably dogged by the trappings of 'civilisation', but are quite agreeable in spite of the unglamorous aspect of warehouses on the opposite side of the burn.

Thankfully, all this is short-lived, as a waymarked path leads you away from the burn to rise across the upper part of the park, which proves to be a pleasantly untidy spread of rough moorland supporting a range of trees, bracken, gorse and tussock grass. A short haul climbs to the first of many vantage points that the Way has in store, a ridge formed from ancient lavas. From it the embryonic panorama captures the suburbs of Glasgow and the Kirkpatrick Hills, and quietly sets the tone for what lies ahead.

From the high point, the Way goes ahead and then left, through more woodland comprised of birch, oak, beech, rowan and gorse. Ignore a branching path on the right, and later turnings at a crosspath, always keeping ahead to enter Mugdock Country Park, a Sensitive Wildlife Area.

As you enter the country park you cross a culverted stream, and then press on through attractive woodland

Gifted in 1980 to the people of Glasgow, Mugdock Wood and the surrounding area of established mixed woodland now forms the Mugdock Country Park, and is an important ecological site, with notable species of flowers, an oak woodland, ruined castles and an attractive loch.

In Mugdock Country Park

29

along the former drive to Craigallian House, flanked on the left by Allander Water. Already the urbanity of Milngavie is forgotten, there is an air of expectancy, and the route is one of pleasurable woodland walking where birdsong invariably helps you on your way.

Ignore a tempting deviation to Mugdock Castle, and keep on instead to leave Mugdock Wood at a lane. Go left, downhill, for a short distance, and then leave the lane, on the right, to enter an area managed by the Loch Lomond Countryside Park Ranger Service.

Mugdock Castle and the Grahams: The Grahams have played an important part in Scottish history, and as you pass through Mugdock so you are striding through the old Barony of Mugdock, centred on Mugdock Castle, the principal seat of the chief of the clan.

Sir John de Graham was of key importance in William Wallace's campaign for the independence of Scotland, while James Graham was a close ally of Rob Roy MacGregor. But it was the 1st Marquis, the 'Great Montrose', who became recognised as one of the finest military strategists the world has seen, following his support for King Charles I.

Mugdock Castle, overlooking the Clyde valley and occupying an easily-defended site, is the place where James Graham, 4th Marquis and 1st Duke of Montrose was born and spent part of his life.

Allander Water, absent for a short while, resumes its pleasant presence, now stepped and providing a few gushing cascades. Boardwalks traverse a marshy area and ease the Way along through scrubland and then below a pine plantation; the pine shortly gives way to a more mixed woodland of larch, oak and beech.

Suddenly, on rounding a bend you get the first glimpse of Dumgoyne at the western end of the Campsie Fells, and soon reach Craigallian Loch, overlooked by Craigallian House, a fine Victorian mansion.

A broad track heads on from the loch for a brief stretch of woodland once more, eventually to reach the first of a number of holiday chalets that were built

continued on
page 33

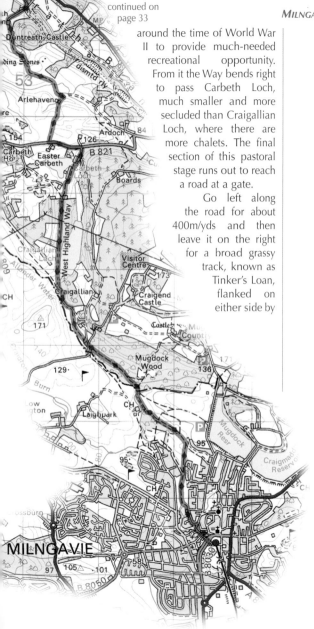

around the time of World War II to provide much-needed recreational opportunity. From it the Way bends right to pass Carbeth Loch, much smaller and more secluded than Craigallian Loch, where there are more chalets. The final section of this pastoral stage runs out to reach a road at a gate.

Go left along the road for about 400m/yds and then leave it on the right for a broad grassy track, known as Tinker's Loan, flanked on either side by dilapidated dykes. The track rises slightly into a stand of beech trees where it ends abruptly at a dyke crossed by a step-stile. Suddenly, as if on an unexpected threshold, from a landscape of relative order and agreeable tranquillity, you gaze out on a vastly different prospect, a rugged, exciting scene that rises to the long line of the Campsie Fells, with the rough escarpment of the Strathblane Hills and the knobbly upthrust of Dumgoyne especially prominent. As if passing through an unseen gateway you move swiftly forward towards the true 'Highland' landscape that is everyone's preconceived notion of the Way, though the great Highland Boundary Fault that 'officially' marks the distinction between lowland and highland Scotland is yet to come.

The end of Tinker's Loan is indeed a threshold for here you step forward from the water catchment of the great Glasgow basin and into Loch Lomond country. The far horizon embraces the rugged Crianlarich hills, a few days away yet and accurately identifiable only by a knowledgeable eye, but attention is inevitably captured by the first glimpse of the much closer bulk of Ben Lomond, the most southerly of the Munros.

The Campsie Fells terminate in the west at Dumgoyne, a conical hill that is by far the most shapely of the Campsies, and stands isolated from the rest. In spite of not being the highest of the Campsie Fells, Dumgoyne, by virtue of its position, commands a fine view of distant Loch Lomond and is popular for that reason alone.

This end of the Campsie Fells overlooks Strath Blane, through which the Way now continues, but before it does it needs to work a way around the wooded volcanic plug of Dumgoyach.

The immediate way on leaves the step-stile to tackle an on-going track that is rocky underfoot, and undulates forward, dropping steadily to a row of cottages known as

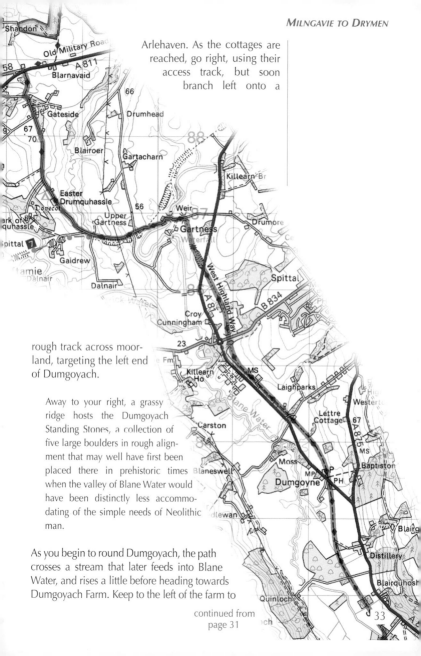

Arlehaven. As the cottages are reached, go right, using their access track, but soon branch left onto a

rough track across moorland, targeting the left end of Dumgoyach.

Away to your right, a grassy ridge hosts the Dumgoyach Standing Stones, a collection of five large boulders in rough alignment that may well have first been placed there in prehistoric times when the valley of Blane Water would have been distinctly less accommodating of the simple needs of Neolithic man.

As you begin to round Dumgoyach, the path crosses a stream that later feeds into Blane Water, and rises a little before heading towards Dumgoyach Farm. Keep to the left of the farm to

continued from page 31

reach a stile and path, with open pasture on the left and a hedgerow on the right. This shepherds you out to meet the farm access, which then descends easily to cross tree-flanked and fast-flowing Blane Water at Dumgoyach Bridge. A few more strides and you leave the access to join the line of a disused railway that will now be your companion and guide for some distance, to near Gartness.

The route of the Blane Valley railway line did not escape the notice of those charged with the responsibility for locating a route for a water pipeline linking Loch Lomond and Central Scotland. With intermittent presence the pipeline, for the most part buried beneath a raised embankment, leads onward and provides an elevated and relatively dry platform during times when the main trackbed is wet.

The line used to be the Blane Valley Railway which was opened with an optimistic, and perhaps opportunistic, eye to an early-day notion of commuter travel, especially when the line was extended northwards to Aberfoyle. The railway was opened in 1867, extended in 1882, saw the loss of passenger services in 1951, and closed completely in 1959.

A series of field access crossings and lanes, all guarded by metal stiles, leads ahead as the Way now plods resolutely onward down Strath Blane. At a clutch of gates there is an invitation to visit the Glengoyne Distillery, founded in 1833, but such blatant temptation would never be seriously considered by dedicated Wayfarers, would it?

Eventually, the Way runs out to meet the A81 at the site of the former Dumgoyne railway station, where the Beech Trees Inn, formerly a village store, offers a timely refreshment halt (opens at 1230 on Sundays).

Go past the pub to a gate giving access to a busy road, turn left for a few strides, then leave the road, right, through a stile (not through a gate) to follow the grassy margin of an elongated field, then by more stiles and a fenced route you resume your close association with the railway trackbed. More stiles, more trackbed, more embankment; it all flows easily onwards to reach a row of cottages. Shimmy right and left through a stile to go behind a small industrial unit manufacturing conservatories, and keep on through a brief wooded passage to reach a back lane.

Cross the lane to a stile, into more sparse woodland, beyond which the proximity of Killearn Sewage Treatment Works may occasionally bring a quickening of the stride that takes you on behind the scruffy rear of a garage, as you parallel the A81.

In due course you reach a farm access to which the Way is briefly diverted, until you can dive through a gate to return to the railway trackbed, and a bout of boggy progress before passing under the B834.

Walkers without time constraints, or who want a short first day, may find Killearn, about 1½km (1 mile) along the B834, a place where accommodation and refreshments may be found.

In Killearn you will also find a monument to George Buchanan (1506–82), a Scottish scholar and humanist, born near Killearn. Educated at a local grammar school, Buchanan was sent, at the age of 14, to study Latin, the language of the Renaissance, at the University of Paris. He came back to Scotland in 1523 and served in the army of the future King James V, later being enrolled at St Andrews as a poor student, before once more visiting Paris, where he taught in the College of Sainte Barbe until 1537.

In 1537, King James appointed him tutor to one of his illegitimate sons, the future Earl of Moray, but found himself standing charged with heresy when a satirical poem about friars offended Cardinal Beaton. Once more Buchanan found himself in France, teaching in Bordeaux (1539–42). In 1547 he was teaching in Coimbra in Portugal when he was arrested by the Inquisition as a suspected heretic. He remained captive for four/six years (records differ), and returned to Scotland only in 1561 to be appointed classical tutor to the 19-year-old Mary, Queen of Scots, in spite of his evident inclination to Protestantism. The queen in due course gave him a sizeable pension, but he later abandoned her cause following the murder in 1567 of Lord Darnley, her husband of 18 months, when Buchanan charged her with complicity.

In 1567, he was elected moderator of the General Assembly of the Church of Scotland, then newly formed, and later became tutor to the four-year-old King James VI.

Buchanan's classic 20-volume *Rerum Scoticarum historia* (1582), became the chief source from which foreigners gleaned their knowledge of Scotland, in spite of its unreliability. He died penniless in Edinburgh having earned a world-wide reputation for his learning and brilliance as a scholar.

The Way presses on from the B834 through pleasant woodland at the rear of cottages, before reaching the A81 once more. Cross the road with care to rejoin the Way, returning to the trackbed. But the track is now coming to an end, as far as Wayfarers are concerned, squeezing along between hawthorn hedgerows as it approaches a bridge where boardwalks lead to wooden steps up to the back road to Gartness. Here you bid farewell to the old Blane Valley railway.

Go left to Gartness, crossing Endrick Water, where some of the individual sandstone cottages emit the evocative smell of burning peat. The lane undulates in a pleasant rambling way, but nevertheless carries a regular flow of traffic of which heavily laden Wayfarers need to be aware.

The onward route now continues in league with the road, climbing westward over the former Forth and Clyde Junction Railway, now an untidy tangle of scrub that has developed since its closure in 1934. From the top of a rise near Upper Gartness Farm there is a splendid view over the farmlands of Strath Endrick and backwards to the landscapes just travelled. It is all extremely peaceful and satisfying.

The road remains your guide as it passes Easter Drumquhassle Farm (where there is a camp site and other accommodation). Steadily the road leads on, past a quarry, and finally starts to descend gently as it heads for Drymen.

Just after a sharp bend, the Way leaves the road, right, down steps to cross a stream, then following a grassy path, climbing initially to a waymark, beyond which the continuation to reach the A811 is obvious. Leave the field by a stile at the top on the left on to the main road, where the Way goes across and to the right.

Walkers bound for Drymen for an overnight stay (which

adds about 1 km/ ½ mile each way) have two possibilities. One, instead of leaving the road following the sharp bend, keep on to meet the A811 a little closer to Drymen, cross it and climb steps to meet a minor lane leading into the village.

Or, having crossed the field, on reaching the A811 turn left and shortly right to follow an alternative way into the village, which has a full range of facilities, a splendid hotel with excellent restaurant and leisure facilities (Buchanan Arms Hotel), and a well-stocked library/information centre, for those for whom the quest for knowledge knows no peace.

Drymen: Drymen stands above Strath Endrick, the name deriving from druim, a ridge or rise, and the lands of Drymen were said to have been given to a Hungarian nobleman. Drymen, like the parish of Killearn passed through earlier in the walk, was also once part of The Lennox, a historical area associated with the Earls of Levenox or Lennox, which once included extensive tracts of Stirlingshire as well as the greater part of Dunbartonshire.

The earliest traces of the Lennox name are obscure, but certainly date from at least the twelfth century, the name being thought to derive from leamhanach, meaning a place among elm trees. The Lennox family were a determined breed, and as Maurice Lindsay comments in *The Lowlands of Scotland*, few of the lords of Lennox 'died with their boots off', reigning over their domain 'with the absolute feudal sway of monarchs, and on more than once occasion, challenged the authority of the King himself'. The fifth earl, Malcolm (1292–1333), was a solid ally of Robert the Bruce during the Wars of Independence, and came to the Bruce's aid when he sought shelter in a cave along Loch Lomond, now known as Rob Roy's Cave.

The direct line of descent ended in 1672 when the Lennox lands and title (now a Dukedom) fell to Charles II, who conferred them on an illegitimate son, the sixth Duke of Lennox, who in turn passed them on to the Marquis of Montrose.

As you reach Drymen so you enter the ancient and very large Parish of Buchanan. In 1621, the lands of Buchanan were annexed into the parish of Inchcailloch, and the parish enlarged so that it extended from west of Stirling to the mouth of the River Endrick, north through the middle of Loch Lomond to Island I Vow, and from there east to the head of Glen Gyle and along the upper water of Loch Katrine before heading back to the Endrick.

Drymen to Balmaha

Distance:	11km (6.9 miles)
Ascent:	350m (1148 feet)

Walkers who stayed overnight in Drymen need first to return to the point at which the Way was abandoned. In early morning sunlight this is a refreshing start to the day, marred, and at that only nominally, by the quirk of route finding that has you heading away from your immediate objective, Conic Hill. But such contrary motion is short lived, as the route returns to a more comfortable setting.

Directly opposite the point at which the Way emerges from the field to meet the A811, you ascend a brief and narrow ramp (signposted) which lifts you to an old section of road. Turn right to a corner, and then pick up a path sandwiched between beech hedgerows, with open pastures and the dark stand of Garadhban Forest away to the left. The hedgerowed path is a brief interlude before the Way pops out to run beside the A811 for a short while. At a signposted stile on the left you leave the

Conic Hill

road, not to see another one (other than very briefly) until you reach Balmaha on the shores of Loch Lomond – quite a comforting thought.

On leaving the road walk ahead along the edge of an open field, very soon being channelled into a gorse-lined lane that emerges into another open field before reaching a stile at the entrance to Buchanan Forest. Press on along a broad track which rises to meet a main forest trail at a waymark, and bears left into the dark embrace of mature conifers, which are gradually being cleared.

Having risen steadily you reach a metal bar across the forest trail and immediately meet a surfaced track. Turn left and descend for a few strides before turning right into Garadhban Forest. Pleasant walking ensues, with fine cameos of distant hills peering above the trees and occasional glimpses of Loch Lomond. The trail starts to descend, but continues to undulate onward for a while, and with numerous burns issuing from the forest, the sound of running water is never far distant.

> In autumn, beneath the canopy, which within strides of the trail seems dark and impenetrable, there are some fine fungal displays. Yet in spite of the denseness of the trees the forest is never oppressive, the Way travelling largely at the top edge of the plantation, and with far blue hills constantly coming and going from view.

Finally the forest trail reaches its end and, at a waymark, turns right to focus its attention on Conic Hill.

> The ensuing stretch over Conic Hill has a number of problems associated with it. It involves a fair amount of ascent (though nothing excessive), so anyone seeking less strenuous passage (or saving themselves for more demanding work alongside Loch Lomond) should follow the forest road left, down to Milton of Buchanan and thence along the road to Balmaha. Secondly, during a four week period through April into May the route over Conic Hill will be closed because of lambing and calving, and walkers are asked to take the alternative route to avoid disturbance of stock. Please note that, as

The A811 lies along the line of a former military road that linked Stirling and Dumbarton, a strategically important line of communication. The road was constructed under the command of Major Caulfield between 1770 and 1784, though it is generally thought that the work amounted to little more than realignment of an existing road; evidence, however, is scant.

in other parts of the West Highland Way, dogs are not allowed on Conic Hill at any time.

As you step forward to leave the forest you are greeted by a splendid view across island-studded Loch Lomond with the hogsback of Conic Hill away to the right, partly screened by trees. Turn towards Conic Hill, when another section of forest trail, through Garadh Ban Wood, takes up the responsibility of leading you on. Eventually, the trail degenerates into a much narrower gravel path ascending

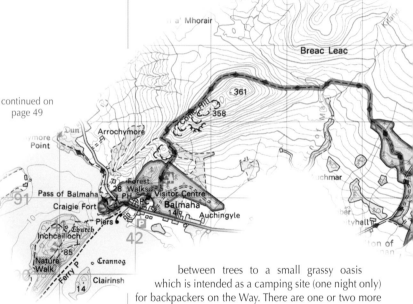

continued on
page 49

between trees to a small grassy oasis which is intended as a camping site (one night only) for backpackers on the Way. There are one or two more of these Forestry Commission sites to come, though they seem a little too oppressive and would not be conducive to sleeping in a tent during or after rainfall, nor suitable for light sleepers.

The path eases on through the forest before finally emerging at a broad stile across a deer fence with open moorland and the bracken-clad flanks of Conic Hill rising away to the left. Loch Lomond again features in the view, and is to be the source of many photographic gems over the next two days or so.

Leaving the forest behind, move on along a wide grassy path flanked by bracken. After a short sweep out on to the moors, the path swings round to begin heading for Conic Hill, preceded by the tree-lined gorge of the Burn of Mar. A good, stony track strides out across the moorland, crossing Killandan Burn, agreeably set in an attractive rowan-lined gorge, by a footbridge, before meeting a fence and stile that gives on to a path running down to the Burn of Mar, an ideal place, among birch and rowan, for a breather and a brew.

Immediately across the Burn of Mar bridge a flight of steps begins the ascent across the flank of Conic Hill, the first significant uphill work of the route. The steps rise steeply through bracken before becoming a less demanding path through heather.

As the path rises, so Ben Lomond comes into view along with Loch Lomond, the

continued from page 33

41

Approaching Conic Hill

Isolated boulders on the top of Conic Hill are probably erratics, left there by the great ice sheet that completely submerged Scotland more than 10,000 years ago.

Luss Hills and distant Ben Vorlich, Ben Vane, Ben Ime and Ben Narnane. There is no scope for missing the way on this ascent, which takes about half an hour to the large cairn just beyond the highest point. The route does not go to the top of Conic Hill, which requires a diversion by a diagonally slanting path from the highest point of the main route, which it is better to retrace, given the steepness of the slopes on the other side and running down to Bealach Ard.

> Conic Hill lies along the Highland Boundary Fault, a great geological divide that traditionally separates lowland Scotland from the highlands. This fault runs for 260km (160 miles) across Scotland from Arran in the west to Stonehaven on the east coast. As you cross Bealach Ard you could well achieve a situation where you have one foot in lowland Scotland and another in the highlands. It is not that simple, of course, but the fault continues through Loch Lomond, and is especially notable on one of its islands, Inchcailloch, about which more anon.

From the highest point, the path descends quite steeply, and in wet conditions requires care. The views improve with every step, and are a constant delight. After the steepest part of the descent the path divides with one arm (the one to follow) crossing the main thrust of the ridge, going left across Bealach Ard, and continuing into a small basin before swinging round to face the fertile plains at the southern end of Loch Lomond where the River Endrick casts about in reluctant loops before resigning itself to the inevitable and finally joining forces with the loch at a sandy spit known as Ring Point.

> The area hereabouts forms part of the Loch Lomond National Nature Reserve and is a real microcosm of wildlife, unique for flowers and widely renowned for its wader and wildfowl populations, especially in winter when hundreds of white-fronted geese arrive from Greenland.
>
> This richness of flora and fauna did not escape the attention of Walter Scott who, in Rob Roy, describes 'a fair and fertile land, [offering] one of the most surprising, beautiful and sublime spectacles in nature'.
>
> The reserve comprises five islands and part of the adjacent mainland. The land, once cleared of forests and drained for commercial use, has now been restored to more natural conditions. Walkers tackling the Way in easy stages may find time to visit one of the islands, Inchcailloch, or even camp overnight on the island (providing you arrange for someone to collect you the next day!).

At the foot of the corrie a right turn takes you on to a narrow ledge above a small ravine, then to descend a steep flight of steps that does nothing for tired or heavily-laden legs and in summer is flanked by bracken and a few goat willow. As the steps end, so the path runs ahead to reach the boundary of forest, the Balmaha Plantation, at a kissing gate.

Beyond, more steps lead down on a woodland path that soon develops to a broad trail descending amid birch and larch to reach a T-junction with another forest trail. Here, turn right.

The plantation is part of the much more extensive Queen Elizabeth Forest Park, and the trail through it guides you out to a large car park at Balmaha. Go directly across the car park to a toilet block and informa-tion panel, before passing on to reach the B837, and the lapping waters of Loch Lomond at Balmaha. Turn right.

Balmaha to Rowardennan

Distance:	12km (7½ miles)
Ascent:	200m (655 feet)

You may be forgiven for thinking the section of the Way from Balmaha to Rowardennan, never far from the great loch, is a gentle riparian ramble. If you do think that, you are in for a shock, for this delightful section of the route squirms its way 'up hill and down dale' as if determined to wring every last ounce of pleasure from the experience. Fresh legs from Balmaha will experience no difficulty; those that have already marched in from Drymen may find some sections a little wearying towards the end of the day.

On a clear day, photographers will be deliriously happy with the opportunities the walk up Loch Lomond provides to take endless pictures; natural historians will encounter a surfeit of reasons to dally, all valid, of course, while those who delight in the simple pleasure of quality walking may just feel disposed to turn round and do it again – well, perhaps not!

Bluebell banks at Loch Lomond

Meaning the village by the water, Balmaha is an immensely popular place with those who find their recreation in boats, and during the summer months especially the village is well populated.

There is evidence that man inhabited the loch islands as long ago as 5000BC, and certainly the tiny island called The Kitchen to the east of Clairinsh is the remains of a crannog, an Iron Age man-made island built about 2000 years ago.

Inchcailloch is a fascinating place, and on it you will find a burial ground associated with a groups of nuns who lived and worshipped on the island following the death in 734 of the female Irish missionary, Saint Kentigerna; she was also mother of Saint Fillan. A church dedicated to the saint was built in the early thirteenth century and this served the area as the parish church until 1621, when worship was transferred to the mainland.

Much of the woodland on Inchcailloch is oak, planted during the early nineteenth century by the Montrose Estate to produce bark for tanning leather. Trees are also a dominant feature of the walk up Loch Lomond, and much of the timber produced was used for shipbuilding, houses and churches, and in the seventeenth century as fuel for smelting iron ore. Alder was used to clog soles and to produce charcoal for gun powder.

The inescapable feature of this section of the walk is, however, the loch itself, Loch Lomond, formerly known as Loch Leven, into which river it flows. The loch was formed by the grinding action of glaciers which chiselled a deep valley and eroded the hill tops. It is 30km (18½ miles) long, 7km (4½ miles) wide at its widest point and covers 71 square km (27½ square miles). Just north of Inversnaid it descends to a depth of 190m (623 feet), while the more southerly section is only about 24m (80 feet) deep.

There are 23 named islands in the loch, though some are very small, and only four of these lie further north than Luss. The loch contains some 16 species of fish, including the almost unique powan, a sea fish which

Walkers staying overnight in Balmaha should seriously consider taking a trip to Inchcailloch, one of five islands managed as a national nature reserve along with Clairinsh, Torrinch, Creinch and Aber Isle and the mouth of the River Endrick. You can make arrangements in Balmaha to be ferried out to the island (and brought back!). Visitors fewer than 10 in number do not need permission to visit the island; for more than that number permits may be obtained (in advance) from Scottish Natural Heritage (see Useful Addresses).

Loch Lomond at Inversnaid

adapted to freshwater life when Loch Lomond was cut off from the sea as the land rose at the end of the Ice Age.

Considering the prominence of this vast sheet of water, the poets have had little to say about it. Wordsworth made a token contribution, and Sir Walter Scott made a few references to the loch and its place in history; but overall its impact on the poetic mind has been singularly unimpressive, with one notable exception, the song *Loch Lomond*. Far from being the 'love' song it might easily be supposed to be, *Loch Lomond* is in fact a Jacobite song, and focuses on the Celtic belief that when a man dies in a foreign land his spirit returns home by the 'low road'. The passion that imbues the song is that of a man yearning for his native land. But one perceptive observation on this topic came from the pen of Maurice Lindsay who, in *The Lowlands of Scotland*, wrote 'One reason for this dearth of written poetry is that the loch and the mountains that close in upon its northern reaches are themselves a kind of poetry: a poetry which alters subtly in form and texture with every wind that swirls around those mist-steamed Highland bens, and varies with every fresh sweep of the sun'. So let's discover the poetry of Loch Lomond for ourselves.

Loch Lomond

The Way continues to the left of a low wall. When this ends, ignore the main road that climbs steeply on the right, but go ahead past a white cottage along a tarmac lane. Soon, at a waymark, you leave the lane and climb a flight of steps into trees. Above the trees the path climbs through bracken banks to reach a horizontal path and a splendid viewpoint, known as Craigie Fort, embracing Loch Lomond and, to the right, Conic Hill, where the line of the Highland Boundary Fault is now particularly noticeable.

Move on by diving into nearby shrubbery to follow a precarious descent on wet rock and over tree roots, eventually reaching the water's edge. When you arrive at an open grassy field (No Camping sign), keep left along its bottom edge to a footbridge in a dip, rising to another field beyond. Much pleasant if circuitous meandering through woodland close to the shoreline leads on round Arrochymore Point and eventually brings you to the shingle beach and car park at Milarrochy.

Keep on between trees along the shingle with fine views across the loch of its islands and the Luss Hills beyond. A short stretch along the road follows before

continued on page 50

continued from page 40

continued on
page 55

you leave it for a footpath on the right-hand side just a few steps away and running parallel with it. The path emerges back on to the road at Blair Bridge but soon leaves it on the left for a western fringe section of the vast Queen Elizabeth Forest Park.

The path is never far from the road, but wanders pleasantly along, eventually crossing a stream before rising a little to a waymark sending you left and immediately right up steps into

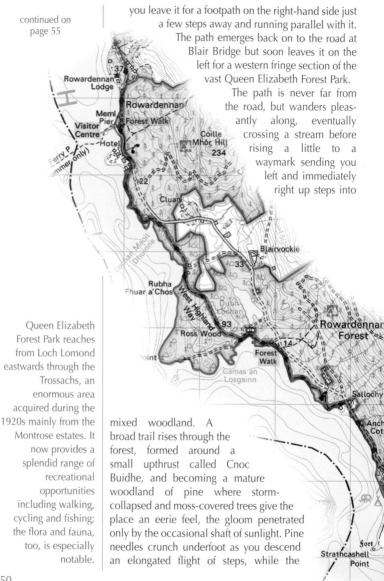

Queen Elizabeth Forest Park reaches from Loch Lomond eastwards through the Trossachs, an enormous area acquired during the 1920s mainly from the Montrose estates. It now provides a splendid range of recreational opportunities including walking, cycling and fishing; the flora and fauna, too, is especially notable.

mixed woodland. A broad trail rises through the forest, formed around a small upthrust called Cnoc Buidhe, and becoming a mature woodland of pine where storm-collapsed and moss-covered trees give the place an eerie feel, the gloom penetrated only by the occasional shaft of sunlight. Pine needles crunch underfoot as you descend an elongated flight of steps, while the shadowy depths and bright interludes are food for an imaginative mind.

Before long the forest trail emerges to rejoin the road near Cashel Farm. Just beyond the Cashel camp site, leave the road and ascend a few stone steps into woodland for a brief diversion that re-emerges onto the road near an old quarry a short distance on. Another brief woodland loop follows immediately before you rejoin the road. Now cross the road to the loch shoreline and set off along a pathway beside a low drystone wall.

Eventually you are forced back on to the road near Sallochy, beyond which, at a waymark, you can ascend, left, into open oak woodland. This woodland is pleasant and leads you down to the loch once more, but a short way on it begins a punishing little climb, including rocky steps, before you cross its highest point. Thankfully, the descent is far less demanding and much more agreeable. This happy interlude continues for some distance, never far from the shores of the loch, and in due course descends to an area to which vehicles have access. When you reach the edge of this, keep ahead on a surfaced track until you can cross a footbridge spanning an inflowing burn.

Beyond the burn the Way pushes on along the shore, passing a university boathouse and field study centre, before moving steeply into Ross Wood. The descending path comes down to a waymark that directs you left along a needle-strewn pathway, finally to burst out into a felled area with a fine view of the mountains across the loch. The Way passes behind a building and reaches the shoreline again, passing a cottage and crossing a burn by a footbridge.

The on-going footpath leads through more woodland to a second footbridge and then goes through a gap in a wall. At the top a splendid view of Ben Lomond and Ptarmigan awaits. With a sense of relief, because there is another steep wooded hill ahead, the path finally drops to the road.

Do not go to the road, but turn left into a cleared area to a waymark at the far side, down stone steps and through tall bracken, almost touching the road again,

Ben Lomond and Loch Lomond

Ben Lomond (974m/3195 feet) is the most southerly of the 276 Munros and is an excellent walk that is worth breaking your journey to tackle. It should require little more than half a day, but its value as a viewpoint is enormous.

but leaving it, left, down more steps to pass round a small inlet within sight of the road. Turn left along a broad forest trail (signposted) to continue the shoreline woodland way.

Finally, between rhododendron bushes, a flight of stone steps briefly rollercoasts up and down until finally, almost unbelievably, you come within site of Rowardennan Pier, being deflected by a fence up to the road. Go left along the road, which leads past the Rowardennan Hotel and the car park used by walkers bound for Ben Lomond, to peter out at the entrance to the youth hostel.

Rowardennan to Crianlarich

Distance:	33km (20½ miles)
Ascent:	450m (1475 feet)

The complete stage from Rowardennan to Crianlarich is one of the longest days if done in its entirety, and though there have been footpath improvements to many stretches, it remains a demanding walk that should not be undertaken lightly, even by strong walkers. The opportunity to break the stage, however, occurs conveniently at a couple of points (Inversnaid and Inverarnan), and there is good sense in doing this if you have the slightest doubt about your ability to tackle the complete trek comfortably.

Between Rowardennan and Rowchoish bothy you have a choice of routes. The easier keeps to a broad forest trail, while a more energetic (but improved) path takes a line closer to the loch shore. Both routes merge a short distance before the end of the broad trail, beyond which excellent walking ensues.

In spite of the ruggedness, the walking throughout is of the highest quality, and there comes a tremendous feeling of satisfaction from coping with the very variable terrain. Towards the end, should you be feeling weary, you can always finish into Crianlarich on the road, and, if you want to be punctilious about following the Way in its entirety, return to the point at which you joined the road the next day.

Head towards (or from) the youth hostel and start up a broad forest trail which soon reaches Ptarmigan Lodge, named after the satellite of Ben Lomond that lies directly above. A short way on past the lodge, the low-level route branches left, down steps, to pursue a shoreline route through oak and birch that gives plenty of scope for adding woodland, loch and mountain pictures to your collection. The path meanders progressively through the woodland and past the Rowchoish bothy before rising to rejoin the main trail. On the way it rounds a crag known as Rob Roy's

Prison, where, according to tradition, he detained prisoners and hostages. Whether that was ever so in reality it another matter, but it serves as a timely reminder that you are now entering the lands of Clan MacGregor.

Romanticised by Sir Walter Scott in the novel that bears his name and more recently given the 'Hollywood' treatment, Rob Roy MacGregor is a figure who still looms large in Scottish history, a man who led an adventurous life with, by all accounts, an unconventional attitude to other people's property. Born in 1671 (some accounts say 1660) in Glengyle, he was the second son of Donald MacGregor of Glengyle, a lieutenant-colonel and chief of a sept (clan) of the MacGregors. Until 1661 the Clan Gregor had for almost a century been pursued with fire and sword during a time when anyone and everyone had not only the right but the duty to slay, harry, burn and dispossess any MacGregors they might find, without recourse to the authorities – always assuming the MacGregors let them. This was later followed by proscription of the name MacGregor so that none might legally call themselves by the name – Rob Roy himself used his mother's name, Robert MacGregor Campbell.

For more than 25 years Rob Roy lived a relatively settled existence at Balquhidder. Nevertheless, his herds were so often plundered that he had to maintain a force of arms to defend himself, expanding this to embrace his neighbours in a seventeenth-century protection racket. With many of his followers espousing the Jacobite cause, Rob Roy decided upon a measure of plundering of his own, and, after having purchased the lands of Inversnaid and Craigroyston, he laid claim to be chieftain of the clan. With mounting losses in cattle speculation, Rob Roy found himself at odds with the Duke of Montrose (from whom he had borrowed money), and so forfeited his lands, his houses were burned down, and his wife and children cast adrift in mid-winter. Open war between Rob Roy and the duke ensued the year after the 1715 rebellion, and a legacy of stories remains of his exploits, narrow escapes, actual escapes when captured, and of his generosity to the poor. In 1727 he was arrested

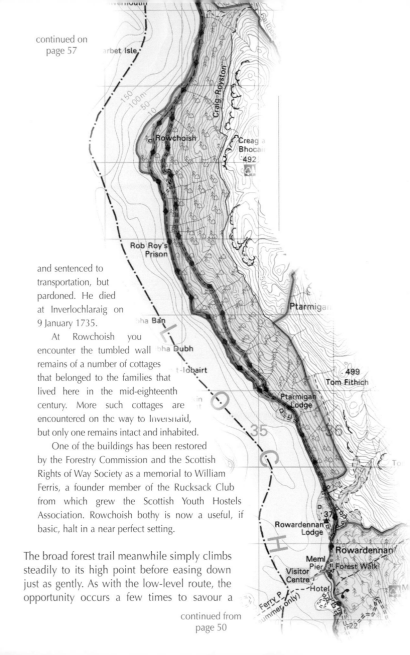

continued on
page 57

and sentenced to
transportation, but
pardoned. He died
at Inverlochlaraig on
9 January 1735.

At Rowchoish you
encounter the tumbled wall
remains of a number of cottages
that belonged to the families that
lived here in the mid-eighteenth
century. More such cottages are
encountered on the way to Inversnaid,
but only one remains intact and inhabited.

One of the buildings has been restored
by the Forestry Commission and the Scottish
Rights of Way Society as a memorial to William
Ferris, a founder member of the Rucksack Club
from which grew the Scottish Youth Hostels
Association. Rowchoish bothy is now a useful, if
basic, halt in a near perfect setting.

The broad forest trail meanwhile simply climbs
steadily to its high point before easing down
just as gently. As with the low-level route, the
opportunity occurs a few times to savour a

continued from
page 50

stunning canvas in which triple-peaked Ben Arthur, better known as The Cobbler, and the nearby Ben Narnain, are portrayed to superb effect.

Within a short distance of the two routes combining, the broad trail comes to an end and collapses into a woodland pathway of considerable pleasure. Oak, birch and pine provoke shifting shadows and dappled delights as you move along, not to mention a continuing downpour long after rain has stopped. At a small burn you reach the base of a bracken-clad slope with fewer trees, but beyond this brief interlude you return to the greenery before finally quitting the Queen Elizabeth Forest Park at the Cailness Burn. Close by stands Cailness Cottage.

You cross Cailness Burn by a large footbridge that stands on the site of at least two previously demolished bridges which were swept aside in 1975 and 1985. The dry conditions of 1995 seem to have allowed the bridge to escape its decadal demolition, and hopefully it will continue to survive.

The Way eases on towards Inversnaid, waymarked whenever it is needed, and passing through pleasant woodland well populated with birdlife. After a few small rises, all lost again, the Way finally rounds a small rock buttress falling into the loch and brings you quite suddenly to the first of two bridges that take you across Snaid Burn and its attractive waterfall to reach the car park of the Inversnaid Hotel.

The on-going stretch of the Way between Inversnaid and Inverarnan has long held a reputation for being the most difficult part of the whole walk. In the mid-1990s, however, some improvements were made to the pathway, now hardly noticeable, and these have significantly eased the difficulties. Even so, it is not the easiest of sections and will require your concentration throughout, especially since it still involves a fair amount of strenuous undulating walking and has a few rocky sections to contend with. Once you start moving away from the loch shore, so these difficulties end, and much easier walking ensues.

Go in front of the Inversnaid Hotel and cross the car

The Inversnaid Hotel operates a boat service across the loch, but it is a private service, not a ferry, primarily for hotel guests, and as such does not operate to a timetable. Close by, Inversnaid Lodge stands in a secluded elevated position overlooking the loch. It was originally built in 1790 as a hunting lodge for the Duke of Montrose.

continued on page 61

park to a WHW signpost, there entering the Royal Society for the Protection of Birds Nature Trail, a further reminder of the wealth of birdlife you can expect to find along this wooded eastern shore of Loch Lomond. You start along a gravel path (in front of a toilet block) that soon enters woodland. A short way on, the route passes a boathouse from where there is a splendid view across the loch of Ben Vorlich, Ben Vane and, further south, Ben Narnain. The Way then rises on a narrow path through bracken to a small burn and footbridge where the RSPB trail climbs to the right and the Way crosses the bridge to the left. (One-night camping is again permitted just here.)

The continuing path tackles a short cliff at the base of which a large tumble of boulders has created the cavern known as Rob Roy's Cave, which will require a brief diversion and some finding amid the confused terrain.

In spite of the cave's association with Rob Roy, who may indeed have used it, there is a claim, too, that it was once named after Robert the Bruce, who is said to have sheltered there following defeats in battle at Methven and Dalrigh.

Beyond the cave the rugged going persists as the Way plunges onward, casting about from gravelly shoreline to boggy woodland stretches. Here, help lies only back the way you came or ahead at Inverarnan, and in poor weather conditions you

continued from page 55

Heading for upper Loch Lomond

can feel very isolated. Nor does the feeling go away for some time, as the route penetrates further up the glen, past a long-abandoned croft at Pollochro, and on to reach the Allt Rostan opposite Island I Vow. Here, at a fence, you leave one county and enter another.

More scrambling progress is needed before, with a delightful sense of relief, the difficulties end on the approach to the open bay a short distance south of Doune. Beyond the burn that flows into the loch at this point, the Way begins an easy and pleasant ascent, keeping largely to open ground as it treks across to Doune, where there are two buildings, one a bothy, the other a restored farmhouse. It is a splendid location, and travellers along the A82 on the far side of the loch must be envious as they look across to the stark white building and the walkers lounging around with evident contentment.

Lochside wandering follows as the route presses on towards Ardleish, just south of which anyone wanting to escape could go down to the shore and hoist a cone to summon a ferry from the other side. Continuing above Ardleish Farm, the Way climbs to cross a small ridge, running on to cross a dyke by a stile, before easing up to a shallow glen to the east of Cnap Mor and down to Dubh Lochan.

> Cnap Mor is something of a threshold on this section of the walk, for it is here that with little or no ceremony you move from what is essentially the Loch Lomond basin into Glen Falloch, its northerly colleague. After so much delightful walking in its company, you bid farewell to the great loch, so you are entitled to express a few appropriate words on the experience!

For a short while the Way seems reluctant to descend from Dubh Lochan, maintaining a lofty air with the trinity of Munros, Beinn Lui, Beinn Oss and Beinn Dubhcraig towering over the moors of Glen Falloch in splendid fashion. Finally, the path does begin to descend, easing companionably through woodland to emerge onto level ground just south of Ben Glas Burn. A bridge leading immediately to a stile finally brings you

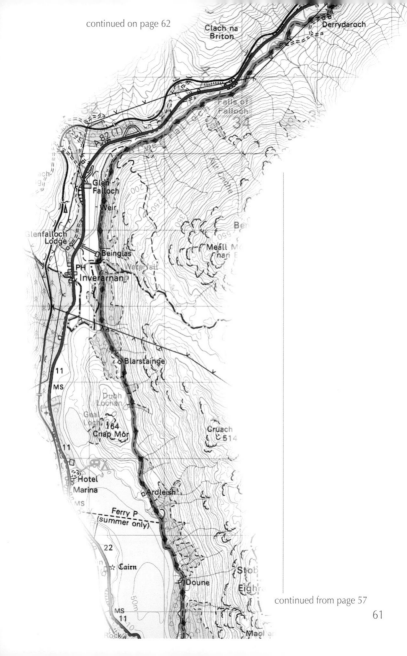

continued on page 62

Clach na
Briton

Derrydaroch

Falls of
Falloch

34

Glen
Falloch

Weir

Glenfalloch
Lodge

Be

Meall M
han E

Beinglas

PH
Inverarnan

Blarstainge

11

MS

Dubh
Lochan

Geal
Loch

164
Cnap Mòr

Gruach
514

Hotel
Marina

11

MS

Ardleish

Ferry P
(summer only)

22

Cairn

Stob

Doune

Eigh

continued from page 57

MS

11

Rocks

Maol

There is considerable overnight accommodation at this stage in the walk. Beinglas Farm itself offers a whole range of facilities from camping (including tent hire) and bunkhouses to B&B, while across the river more facilities await.

to Beinglas Farm; above the bridge the Ben Glas Burn often performs a series of spectacular falls and slides, though they are not best seen from the Way.

This was once a passage well used by drovers, and the Inverarnan Hotel is a former cattle drovers' inn. Traditionally, drovers would meet at the northern end of Loch Lomond, and while the Crieff tryst flourished, Glen Falloch was the quickest way of joining the route from Skye, at the top of Glendochart. Once the Falkirk tryst assumed prominence, around 1770, the route up Glen Falloch saw much less traffic. Another route crossed the River Falloch near this point and traversed the hills to the east of Ardlui to reach Glen Gyle. In A Tour in the Highlands in 1803 James Hogg, the Ettrick shepherd, described using this route for droving sheep.

For the final stage of this section to Crianlarich, the Way runs up Glen Falloch and over a broad, low col into Strath Fillan. Glen Falloch is a splendid continuation of the Way, a complete contrast with what has gone before. The glen river, which is your companion for a while, is a succession of cascades, white-water hollows and rapids, and after heavy rain is an especially fearsome sight. The terrain is a constantly changing scene of open moorland pastures and wooded stands of birch, oak and rowan, and is never dull for a moment.

On reaching Beinglas Farm, having crossed the stile, bear right to another stile at the foot of a path that steeply climbs the hillside above and is a popular route to Beinn Chabhair. Ignore this tempting diversion, and go left along a broad stony access track until, as you approach the main road, you can leave the track, branching right on a rocky path. With a little rough going in the wooded areas, the Way generally continues uneventfully on its journey, passing ruined cottages at Blackcroft that wishful thinking might have you believing is Derrydarroch. For a while, the onward line is a little

continued from page 61

doubtful if you don't spot the tall waymark at a bridge. But beyond that, a much more substantial track leads on and eventually down to Derrydarroch, sheltered in a little hollow.

Immediately after Derrydarroch cross the Falloch at Derrydarroch Bridge and turn right to traverse a small birch-clad hillock before descending to a constructed path running parallel with the river. About 1km (fi mile) from Derrydarroch the path swings left and passes under the railway line by a low cattle creep, an inelegant and strenuous experience for walkers with large packs. With far greater simplicity than any written description can render, the Way, ignoring steps just beyond the railway, joins the old road for a while and then works round to pass beneath the modern A82 by a tunnel to steps that

As you progress up the glen so the incidence of isolated pine trees grows. These are remnants of the great ancient Caledonian pine forest that covered this entire area following the last Ice Age.

continued on page 66

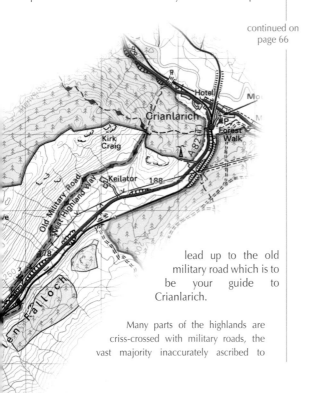

lead up to the old military road which is to be your guide to Crianlarich.

Many parts of the highlands are criss-crossed with military roads, the vast majority inaccurately ascribed to

General Wade. In reality it was his sometime Inspector of Roads, Major William Caulfield, who supervised the construction of many of the roads, notably from 1740, when General Wade left Scotland, until his death in 1767. It was Caulfield who was responsible for all the military roads used by the West Highland Way, and his contribution amounted to something above 1300km (800 miles).

In spite of all his efforts, Major Caulfield was destined to live in the shadow of the general, and even today you hear people speaking of Wade roads when referring to roads built by Caulfield. Caulfield, in truth, built three times as many roads as General Wade, but always gave the general full credit as the originator of the concept. Even so, it is probably fairer to say that Caulfield's work made a greater impact on the communication network in Scotland than anyone.

Beyond the A82, the line of the old military road rises steadily above the glen as it passes Keilator Farm before reaching a stile and meeting of pathways at the edge of the woodland to the west of Crianlarich, where you have a number of choices.

The on-going route here turns left. The most direct way of reaching the main road is ahead, down the initially squelchy Bogle Glen. It is more usual, however, for Wayfarers to take a break at Crianlarich, and by turning right at the stile you follow a steadily descending path through woodland, with fine views of Ben More, Stobinian and Cruach Ardrain, which emerges on the A82 at a rough car park close by the railway station. Walkers bound for the youth hostel or village centre should take the path that goes under the railway line.

As you reach and cross the stile at the head of Bogle Glen, so you step for the first of four times across the British watershed; to the south the waters drain into the Loch Lomond catchment, to the north they are part of the Tay system and flow ultimately into the North Sea.

Crianlarich to Tyndrum

Distance:	10.5km (6½ miles)
Ascent:	120m (395 feet)

Crianlarich lies at the place where traditional through-routes west–east and north–south meet, and rests forever in the shadow of Ben More, along the southern flank of Strath Fillan. It is a village of perpetual activity that largely owes its present-day prominence to its railway connections, an unavoidable location for motorised and railway travellers bound for the Western Highlands and beyond, and splendidly placed for walkers intent on gathering the great summits of the Southern Highlands. The village offers a wide range of B&B facilities, while the youth hostel must rank among the best run in the catalogue of the SYHA.

It is not clear how the name of the village derives. Some authorities suggest it is from Craobh an Iairig, meaning the tree by the pass, and while on the face of it this seems logical, much would depend on how long the name has been in use since much of this area was part of the Caledonian pine forest. It would seem unusual then to single out one tree for special attention.

Crianlarich also has the added attraction for Wayfarers of being roughly half way, with by common consensus the more difficult part already completed – but accept that comment advisedly as the West Highland Way has its own repertoire of dirty tricks, some of which are played out on Rannoch Moor and across the rugged countryside that leads down to and on from Kinlochleven. Do not be lulled into thinking everything is now a few days' easy walking.

En route to Tyndrum the West Highland Way casts about on both sides of Strath Fillan, as if trying to take in all the best bits, in which quest it undoubtedly succeeds. Any preconceived notion that the section begins with densely-packed woodland will be instantly dispelled for the Way threads a course through the trees that provides a host of enticing vistas and a fine balcony walk high above the glen.

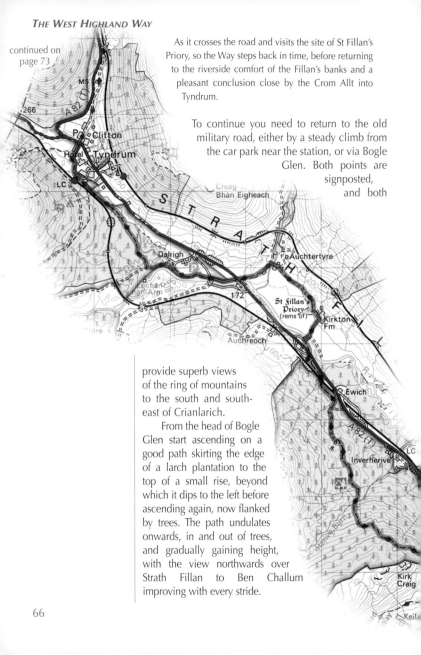

continued on
page 73

As it crosses the road and visits the site of St Fillan's Priory, so the Way steps back in time, before returning to the riverside comfort of the Fillan's banks and a pleasant conclusion close by the Crom Allt into Tyndrum.

To continue you need to return to the old military road, either by a steady climb from the car park near the station, or via Bogle Glen. Both points are signposted, and both provide superb views of the ring of mountains to the south and south-east of Crianlarich.

From the head of Bogle Glen start ascending on a good path skirting the edge of a larch plantation to the top of a small rise, beyond which it dips to the left before ascending again, now flanked by trees. The path undulates onwards, in and out of trees, and gradually gaining height, with the view northwards over Strath Fillan to Ben Challum improving with every stride.

For a while the path effects a pleasant promenade high above the glen, and gradually works a way down to cross Herive Burn by a wooden footbridge. Eventually the path rises to join a broader forest trail at a waymark, with the route here branching right, and it is here that the retrospective view now embraces Stobinian which hitherto had sheltered coyly behind intervening heights. When the on-going track bends to the right, branch left at a waymark, onto a narrow path through a pleasant spread of broom, beside a stream. The path is ultimately deflected right by the Allt an t-Saoir and runs down through larch to pass beneath the railway bridge on the Oban line. Beyond the bridge you reach the old glen road, turning left along it to cross the burn and on to a gravel track leading out to the present-day road.

Cross the main road and go instantly left along a narrow path above a wooded embankment. The path leads to a stile, beyond which the Way diagonally crosses a pasture to reach the bridge spanning the River Fillan. Now the Way runs up towards Kirkton Farm, turning left just before reaching it to swing round to the site of St Fillan's Priory.

St Fillan's Priory was probably a twelfth-century monastic site to the memory of the saint, an Irish monk, son of St Kentigerna, about whom many tales have been handed down of his exemplary life during the eighth century.

Not too far away is the battle site of Dalrigh, where Robert the Bruce suffered a defeat in 1306. It was following this that he granted the monastic settlement the status of priory, logically, it might be assumed, because he received spiritual support from the monks following his defeat. The true site of the priory is thought to be closer to the Holy Pool a short distance upriver.

The most widespread of the tales about St Fillan concerns a sign given to Bruce as he prepared for the Battle of Bannockburn. The accounts tell how a relic of the saint, an arm-bone in

continued from page 63

The Holy Pool is said to be the original site of St Fillan's Priory, and the place where insane persons were bathed in the chilly waters before being taken to the chapel to be tied up all night to the font, a treatment that also involved St Fillan's bell being placed over the head of the person. No records seem to exist to suggest that the treatment actually cured anyone, other than perhaps those who feigned insanity and considered that a sudden recovery of their senses seemed a better proposition.

silver, had been brought to the battlefield as a token of good fortune. As Bruce kneeled, praying before it, the case opened to reveal the relic, much to the astonishment of its guardian who sensibly had brought only an empty case to Bannockburn.

From the priory, cross a cattle grid and branch left on a broad track that runs on to Auchtertyre Farm, beyond which you cross the Allt Auchtertyre and turn left to walk out to rejoin the A82, near the Holy Pool.

Cross the road, and press on down a rough track that is soon accompanied by the river. The path swings round to reach a surfaced lane near a bridge. Walk straight across the lane (waymark), and keep going on a track parallel with the river. On crossing an inflowing stream immediately branch right on a path, which for a short while pursues a very pleasant course beside the river before branching right again on a broad track, which very soon it leaves for a path on the left that cuts across a boggy corner to meet another broad track going left. The Way comes down to cross the Crom Allt by a wooden bridge, near the site known as Dal Righ, the King's Field.

It was at Dal Righ that Robert the Bruce is said to have engaged the MacDougalls of Lorne in battle, when he was defeated. This occurred during an unhappy period, in 1306, following closely on his crowning as King of Scotland, when he was also defeated by English forces at Methven, near Perth, as a result of which he took to the hills with a small group of supporters.

Press on with the track for a short distance until you can leave it, on the right, at a waymark, for a narrow, stony footpath, that rises to pass a small lochan and rambles on uneventfully to reach a derelict area, just beyond which, at a gate, you approach the edge of the developed area that has grown around Tyndrum. A waymark directs you up into woodland for the last serious encounter with trees until the final stages of the walk, and on beside the river to a bridge.

Do not cross the bridge, unless staying at the camp site there, but press on to reach a group of cottages and a surfaced lane. Turn left on reaching the lane (though by turning right you reach the facilities of Tyndrum a little quicker than by following the Way), and follow this round towards Lower Tyndrum Station, leaving it, on the right before reaching the station, for a path doubling towards the river and heading towards Tyndrum. A brief encounter with a shallow burn may impose a moment of wetness before you can stroll up in front of cottages to reach the main road.

Tyndrum to Glencoe

Distance:	30km (18¾ miles)
Ascent:	365m (1200 feet)

Once mistakenly thought to have been one of the highest inhabited villages in northern Britain, Tyndrum has grown enormously (some would say out of all proportions) in the 30-plus years I have been visiting the Highlands.

Tyndrum, the house on the ridge, was an eighteenth- and nineteenth-century service station much favoured by cattle drovers, one of a number of overnight rest halts, or 'stances', usually at intervals of ten miles, encountered along what is now the West Highland Way; others were Inveroran and Altnafeadh at the entrance to Glencoe. Little seems to have changed, for Tyndrum is still very much a resting place on the Highland tourist route, and only those with eyes for the hills seem to look upon the village as anything more than a single night's halt.

Between Tyndrum and the King's House Hotel at the eastern end of Glencoe, the Way provides the opportunity to stride out purposefully across Rannoch Moor, either with the old Glencoe road or one of Caulfield's military roads underfoot. On one hand, the moor itself slips away into the endless blue oblivion of the eastern horizon, on the other, a stunning wall of mountains is your constant shepherd, guiding you easily along the broad trail, yet at the same time a blatant and beguiling temptation to escape into the tantalising summits of Black Mount.

The walking is easy throughout, but the section should not be underestimated. On Rannoch Moor you reach a point as far away from civilisation as anywhere else on the Way, and in poor weather conditions it can be one of the most inhospitable places in Scotland.

From Tyndrum to Bridge of Orchy the main land uses are the growing of trees in plantations and the raising of sheep and cattle. Beyond Forest Lodge at the western end of Loch Tulla, grass and heather dominate the landscape. This is red deer country, and while the deer graze high during the summer months, it is in early spring and late autumn that you stand a good chance of seeing them at lower levels.

The first stage of the journey to Glencoe follows a stretch of the Caulfield road network as far as Forest Lodge, and is seldom far from either the glen road or the seemingly ubiquitous railway. It is a relaxing start, if you stayed overnight in Tyndrum, though many walkers prefer to begin this section at Crianlarich, when the easy walking will be much appreciated in the second half of the day.

Picking up the trail at the main road, go ahead up a surfaced lane beside a burn. When the lane ends, a broad stony track rises up the glen to a gate and stile, running close to the A82 for a while. It presses on, never far from the road, and climbs very steadily to reach the regional boundary at another gate and stile, once more crossing the British watershed.

From the stile keep to the path, which moves slightly to the right beneath the southern slopes of Beinn Odhar, and with the shapely cone of Beinn Dorain directly ahead, set against the farther heights of Black Mount.

The track continues to ascend for a short while, and then levels before beginning the long descent into Auch Gleann (more correctly Gleann Ach'-innis Chailein). Before long the track drops steeply to the left to cross beneath the railway line, beyond which it joins a broader track leading down from the main road near the watershed.

Walking forward into the glen you get a tremendous, invigorating sense of openness and freedom, with the great sweeping sides of Beinn Dorain to draw the eye. Gradually the path descends to a farm, close by which you cross the glen river, the Allt Kinglass, by a single-arch bridge. Over the bridge, turn left on a farm track. A short way on a small wooded riverside glade invites a break, before resuming the trek below the high crags and gullies of Beinn Dorain on the way to Bridge of Orchy Station. There can be no error of route finding

During the mid-1990s a new prosperity loomed large for Tyndrum, that of gold extraction, for the hills had long been known to contain the precious metal. The prospect of extracting 11 grammes of gold per ton of ore, significantly more than most South African gold mines, aroused investment and the hope that the people of Tyndrum would benefit as a result.

Beinn Odhar from the Watershed, north of Tyndrum

continued on
page 75

here: the glen is high, wide and handsome, and the way forward clear enough to follow on the darkest of nights.

When the track reaches Bridge of Orchy Station, branch left at a waymark sign through a metal gate and under the railway to reach a road. Having travelled in the company of the railway since Glen Falloch, the Way now abandons the line, which it will not meet again before journey's end at Fort William. With a similar desire to shun the transport trappings of modern society, the Way shortly quits the main road, which it will not rejoin until it reaches the entrance to Glencoe.

Turn right and go down the lane past the post office to reach the main road opposite the Bridge of Orchy Hotel. Cross the road, and stay on the lane that runs down beside the hotel to cross the River Orchy by a substantial bridge, built around 1750. Anyone who chances by here when the Orchy is at its most turbulent cannot fail to marvel at the ingenuity of the bridge engineers in overcoming the problems the river would have posed.

Between Bridge of Orchy and the start of the crossing of Rannoch Moor lies a brief woodland interlude followed by a stunning descent to Inveroran and Forest Lodge at the western end of Loch Tulla. Tired walkers can simply follow the road, but the climb to Màm Carraigh at the northern end of Ben Inverveigh is nothing like

continued from page 66

William and Dorothy Wordsworth, in company with a southbound cattle drove, stayed at the Inveroran Hotel in September 1803, though they were less than complimentary about the food they received there. Even so, Dorothy was moved to write evocatively of the inn filled with 'seven or eight travellers, probably drovers, with as many dogs, sitting in a complete circle round a large peat fire in the middle of the floor, each with a mess of porridge in a wooden vessel on his knee'.

as difficult as might be supposed, and any weariness you may experience is offset in great measure by a panorama of towering summits that improves with every upward step, reaching a climax at the top of the pass. The view of Stob Gabhar, Stob Choire Odhair and their attendants alone more than justifies this modest little climb.

Leave the road at a waymark and ascend on an initially boggy path rising easily into woodland. When the path breaks free at the top of the forest it swings to the left, still rising at a comfortable gradient, with the view to the east dominated by Beinn Dorain and Beinn an Dothaidh. Onward, the path (the old military road), rises amid grassy hillsides studded with heather. As it climbs so the path swings around and begins a pleasant traverse of the northern hillside of Ben Inverveigh, with excellent views away to the right, of Loch Tulla. Finally, as it crosses a shoulder, a large cairn at the end of the ridge on the right provides a splendid viewpoint of the loch, Forest Lodge and the sprawling mass of granite mountains beyond. Photographers will find that another cairn and a single rowan tree just below the top of the ridge offer an attractive foreground to go with that amazing background.

On the old military road from Mam Carraigh to Forest Lodge

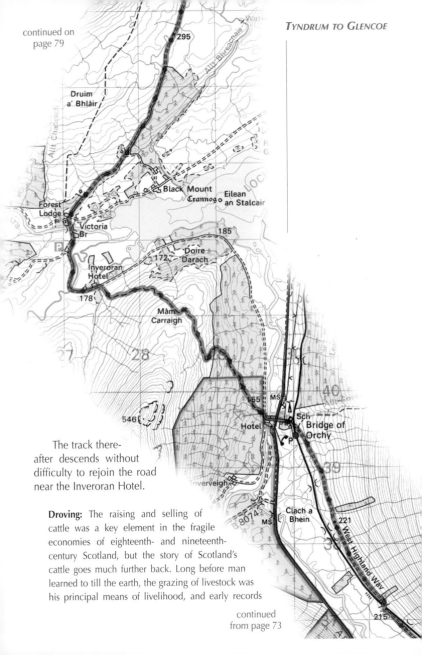

continued on
page 79

The track there-
after descends without
difficulty to rejoin the road
near the Inveroran Hotel.

Droving: The raising and selling of
cattle was a key element in the fragile
economies of eighteenth- and nineteenth-
century Scotland, but the story of Scotland's
cattle goes much further back. Long before man
learned to till the earth, the grazing of livestock was
his principal means of livelihood, and early records

continued
from page 73

The River Ba

bear testimony to the vast numbers of sheep and cattle in Scotland and the importance of grazing.

Breeding and raising cattle was difficult enough, but selling them had its own problems since there were few markets and most of these lay many miles away – in Falkirk and Doune, for example. As the cattle business developed during the eighteenth and nineteenth centuries, the only way to get cattle to market was to walk them there under the experienced eye of teams of drovers. From origins as distant as the Outer Hebrides, Skye, Mull and Ardnamurchan, the cattle would be brought to the southern markets, via Spean Bridge and Fort William, before heading for Kingshouse, Rannoch Moor, Inveroran and Tyndrum. A good part of the West Highland Way pursues these ancient droving routes, so it is fitting that they should be perpetuated in this way.

One curious feature of the droving was the 'shoeing' of cattle, a necessity carried out in just the same way that today we shoe horses. The idea of shoeing cattle just to get them to market may seem strange, but lame cattle were unlikely to command the best prices, assuming they reached the market at all.

Heading for Glencoe

continued on page 81

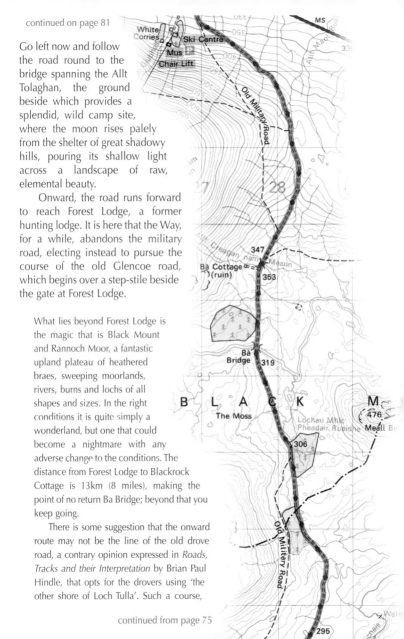

Go left now and follow the road round to the bridge spanning the Allt Tolaghan, the ground beside which provides a splendid, wild camp site, where the moon rises palely from the shelter of great shadowy hills, pouring its shallow light across a landscape of raw, elemental beauty.

Onward, the road runs forward to reach Forest Lodge, a former hunting lodge. It is here that the Way, for a while, abandons the military road, electing instead to pursue the course of the old Glencoe road, which begins over a step-stile beside the gate at Forest Lodge.

What lies beyond Forest Lodge is the magic that is Black Mount and Rannoch Moor, a fantastic upland plateau of heathered braes, sweeping moorlands, rivers, burns and lochs of all shapes and sizes. In the right conditions it is quite simply a wonderland, but one that could become a nightmare with any adverse change to the conditions. The distance from Forest Lodge to Blackrock Cottage is 13km (8 miles), making the point of no return Ba Bridge; beyond that you keep going.

There is some suggestion that the onward route may not be the line of the old drove road, a contrary opinion expressed in *Roads, Tracks and their Interpretation* by Brian Paul Hindle, that opts for the drovers using 'the other shore of Loch Tulla'. Such a course,

continued from page 75

however, would not feed the drove into Inveroran, which was known to be a principal overnight halt. But what is known is that much of the old Glencoe road across Rannoch was improved and maintained by Telford, who may well have found himself with the unenviable responsibility of bringing about a planned road across Rannoch from Killin to Spean Bridge, thankfully a proposal that is still securely filed away, or, hopefully, lost for all time.

Across Rannoch the old military road keeps to the higher ground to avoid the many bogs that would have bedevilled the lower route.

The continuation starts through a small gathering of pine before beginning an unrelenting uphill haul to the first of two high points. Here, on the threshold of the vast Coire Ba, you cross

the British watershed for the penultimate time, before easing down, past Lochan Mhic Pheadair Ruaidhe, to reach the splendidly turbulent River Ba. This is probably the most remote spot on the West Highland Way, a perfect place for a break beneath great craggy summits, scree-riven gullies and the far hills of Achaladair.

A short way on from Ba Bridge the track passes, on the left, the remains of Ba Cottage, surely one of the most isolated shielings imaginable, nestling close by the Allt Creagan nam Meann. A hundred or so strides further and you pass a track that leads out across the southern slopes of Beinn Chaorach to the A82, a marginally shorter way of reaching the road in an emergency than continuing along the Way.

Steadily, the route rises again for its final crossing of the watershed, which it does not far from a prominent cairn, perched on the hillside to the left, to the memory of Peter Fleming, brother of novelist Ian Fleming, who died nearby in 1971.

Now the track becomes less consistent, curves round the massive sprawling flanks of Meall a'Bhuiridh, and starts descending below the White Corries to join the chairlift access road near Blackrock Cottage. Here the Way turns right and marches out to rejoin the A82, briefly, as it crosses the busy road, and presses on down a degenerating surfaced track that leads unerringly to the King's House Hotel.

There is about the whole of this crossing of Rannoch Moor one peculiar and delightfully idiosyncratic aspect, which is the complete

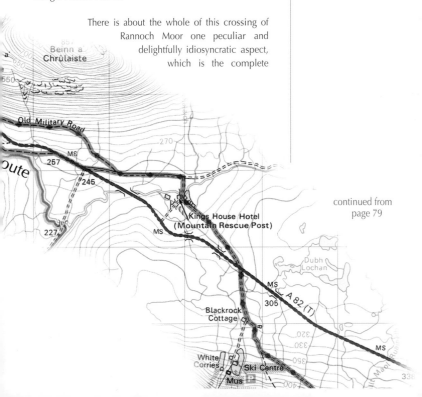

continued from page 79

Kingshouse

The first Caledonian pine forest fire was instigated mainly by the Vikings and warring clans, the latter by the English and Scots who felled the woodlands for iron smelting and to root out wolves and freebooters. There are now very few remnants of that ancient forest, though some will be found around Loch Tulla and yet more at the Black Wood of Rannoch.

absence of any moment when suddenly the scenery becomes wonderful or stunning or breathtaking. Between Loch Tulla and Glencoe it seems that every step of the way you are part of the scenery and the scenery is part of you. No amount of clever words will ever suffice to describe the experience; you must see it for yourself, and form your own impression.

The landscape is also mightily enhanced by a host of lochs and lochans of all shapes and sizes that add constantly changing colour to the scene, from the darkest blacks to the brightest blues. In the breeding season the lochs are visited by many species of wildfowl including black-throated divers, the comparatively rare red-throated divers and greenshanks. Much of the area was once concealed within the great Caledonian pine forest, the Old Wood of Caledon, which formerly extended from Glencoe to Braemar and from Glen Lyon to Glen Affric. Then it was home to a rather more lethal form of wildlife than at present, a place where brown bear, wild boar and wolves were to be found, along with the freebooters who sought sanctuary in the forest.

Much of the great Caledonian pine forest was destroyed by intentional fire and felling firstly between the ninth and twelfth centuries, and later between the fifteenth and eighteenth centuries.

Today, it is all a far cry from those hazardous days when much depended on your skill in coping with a difficult and dangerous terrain, and understanding the secret ways of the mountains and moors. For those who can experience the sensation, it is along the West Highland Way, and this traverse of Rannoch in particular, that you come as close as you can get to being at one with the hills. Make the most of it.

The King's House Hotel: The story of the King's House Hotel goes back perhaps 200 years or more. Certainly, in spite of its remoteness, it was at a key location along the highland drove roads, a fact readily recognised both by the government of the day and those potential innkeepers who were expected to man it. As a result the innkeeper, seemingly loathe to take on such an isolated responsibility, ran the premises rent free and received a substantial government grant for his efforts. By all accounts, however, the innkeeper's efforts were not much to write home about. One traveller who visited the hotel in 1791 described it as having 'not a bed fit for a decent person to sleep in nor any provisions but what are absolutely necessary for the family'. A surveyor of military roads in 1802 complained that it had 'more the appearance of a hog stye than an Inn', while Dorothy Wordsworth, who later had pleasant things to say about the Inveroran Hotel, found the King's House 'a wretched place – as dirty as a house after a sale on a rainy day'. J H B Bell in *Bell's Scottish Climbs* describes conditions at the King's House as 'primitive', where you could 'smell the bacon frying through a hole in the floor' or occasionally had to 'put up an umbrella in bed if the weather was wet'.

So, of the King's House you make what you will. It cannot be avoided, unless you keep on walking.

Glencoe to Kinlochleven

Distance:	14.5km (9 miles)
Ascent:	175m (1230 feet)

The next stage on the Way leads towards the great maw of Glencoe, a glen made eternally famous (or would infamous be more appropriate?) by tales of the massacre of Glencoe (1692), so well and often poignantly described by John Prebble in *Glencoe*. His book, and likewise John Buchan's *The Massacre of Glencoe*, are essential reading for anyone who wishes to absorb the essence of the highlands, and the story of Glencoe in particular. The tale itself reflects an unhappy period in highland life, when most members of the Clan MacDonald were slaughtered by a body of soldiers under Captain Campbell after twelve days of professed friendship, all because of the clan chief's loyalty to the exiled James VII, which brought about a belated submission of the chief and his clan to William and Mary.

In spite of a poor reputation, the ascent of the Devil's Staircase, which takes you out of Glencoe, is not at all difficult. The 'road' was probably constructed around 1750, by Major Caulfield's force, and it seems likely that it was the troops that gave the upper section of the route its name; certainly it is only the top, zigzagging section that is properly called the Devil's Staircase, though the name seems to have been purloined by the whole stretch from Altnafeadh. What is intriguing about the Devil's Staircase route is why it came into being at all, since Caulfield could so easily have gone around the hills to the east and avoided the climb altogether. Both this pass and, further on, the Lairig Mor were finally abandoned for military purposes in 1785 when the longer but easier road through Glencoe to the ferry at Ballachulish was introduced.

On reaching the King's House Hotel turn right on a surfaced lane, passing by a camping area to meet a T-junction. Turn left, still on the surfaced lane, and keep along it to a waymark before rejoining the A82, turning right off the lane onto the old military road once more.

From this point until as far as Altnafeadh there is an alternative route that keeps on to the A82 and thereafter follows the course of the River Coupall for a while.

There is little or nothing between the routes for distance. Both have sections perilously close to the A82 (which carries high-speeding traffic), and both have their attractions. The original line, however, tends to give a better perspective of that great sentinel of Glencoe, Buchaille Etive Mor, which first hove into view as you came down from Rannoch Moor below White Corries and which largely dominates the scene until you disappear over the Devil's Staircase. This alternative is described below.

Buchaille Etive Mor is a summit, now owned and managed by the National Trust for Scotland, that has inspired generations of rock climbers since the days (and before) when W H Murray wrote '...the most striking moment was turning a corner of the road and seeing the great shape, black and intimidating, suddenly spring up

Everything W H Murray says about Buchaille Etive Mor is true. The sudden appearance of the Buchaille as you begin the long run into Glencoe is always an impressive and stirring sight. He goes on to describe 'cliffs dove-grey and terra-cotta', adding that only from a distance is the Buchaille black. On a clear, frosty morning its bulk is the most captivating and memorable of sights.

Crossing Rannoch Moor

in the moor. I had never seen a hill like it before and my breath was taken away from me'. He is, of course, describing the vision you will receive, at a more leisurely pace, as you approach White Corries.

Glencoe, setting aside its nefarious history and the blemishes that modern tourism have inflicted upon it, remains a superlative glen, long, steep-sided, rugged, dark, mysterious, and rising from the often turbulent waters of countless burns and rivers. In the Gaelic tongue, the name signifies Glen of Weeping, yet in spite of any lyricism I may heap upon it, it was regarded by Lord Macaulay in his *History of England* as 'the most dreary and melancholy of all the Scottish passes – the very Valley of the Shadow of Death'. It is not clear whether in making this comparison Lord Macaulay had actually visited all the other Scottish passes, but he was far from happy with Glencoe. 'Mists and storms brood over it through the greater part of the finest summer,' he wrote, 'and even on those rare days when the sun is bright, and when there is no cloud in the sky, the impression made by the landscape is sad and awful. Mile after mile the only sound that indicates life is the faint cry of a bird of prey from some storm-beaten pinnacle of rock.'

Having left the surfaced lane at the waymark, a rough track now rises onto the moor to begin a horizontal traverse below the slopes of Beinn a'Chrulaiste, with the forward view and that to the summits of Black Mount always inspiring.

Gradually the track descends to cross a roadside fence and to run parallel on a graded track with the A82 for a short distance before recrossing the fence and heading for the stand of pine trees at Altnafeadh. A short way on, another fence crossing takes you on to a path that gradually descends to road level, passing around sheep pens, as the great glen, Lairig Gartain, between Buchaille Etive Mor and its sibling Buchaille Etive Beag, eases into view. Eventually the path does come down to the road and for a short but hazardous distance the Way runs beside the A82. Shortly, as it reaches the Altnafeadh, the Way leaves the road, dipping to the right

continued on
page 95

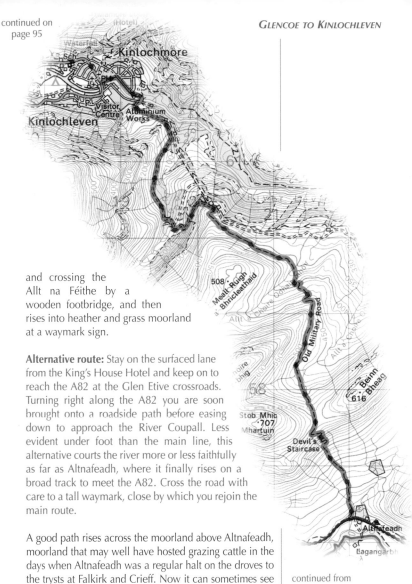

and crossing the
Allt na Féithe by a
wooden footbridge, and then
rises into heather and grass moorland
at a waymark sign.

Alternative route: Stay on the surfaced lane
from the King's House Hotel and keep on to
reach the A82 at the Glen Etive crossroads.
Turning right along the A82 you are soon
brought onto a roadside path before easing
down to approach the River Coupall. Less
evident under foot than the main line, this
alternative courts the river more or less faithfully
as far as Altnafeadh, where it finally rises on a
broad track to meet the A82. Cross the road with
care to a tall waymark, close by which you rejoin the
main route.

A good path rises across the moorland above Altnafeadh,
moorland that may well have hosted grazing cattle in the
days when Altnafeadh was a regular halt on the droves to
the trysts at Falkirk and Crieff. Now it can sometimes see
droves of a different order, those of laden Wayfarers

continued from
page 80

89

Blackrock Cottage, Black Mount, Glencoe

bound for Kinlochleven. The route steadily gains height, and brings improving views of the summits of Glencoe and Black Mount, with the latter now becoming more distant. Finally, with zigzags taking the sting out of the tail of the ascent, you cross a cairned gap between Beinn Bheag and Stob Mhic Mhartuin, the highest point of the West Highland Way at 548m (1798 feet).

> On a clear day the view from the gap is outstanding, especially to the north where you have your first glimpse of Ben Nevis, Carn Mor Dearg and the Mamores. Ahead and below you lies a great boggy bowl drained by the Allt a'Choire Odhair-bhig, which feeds into the River Leven not far from the dam on the Blackwater Reservoir.

The Blackwater Reservoir was one of the last great engineering feats undertaken by the itinerant gangs of navvies who were responsible over many years for most of Britain's canals, roadways and railways. The dam, almost a kilometre (fi mile) wide, was constructed between 1905 and 1909 and produced a reservoir that extends eastwards for 13km (8 miles). It provided water for the aluminium works at Kinlochleven.

Before plunging down to the Allt a'Choire Odhair-bhig, the Way takes a relaxing moment at the top of the Staircase. As you descend, it is as if you are shutting out the delights of the earlier part of the Way, and very distinctly entering a new stage. Grass and heather, punctuated by bouldery outcrops, predominate as a rocky path sweeps down to the burn before slipping across the northerly end of a narrow ridge, Sron a'Choire Odhair-bhig, which if followed westwards would take you on to the narrow and spectacular Aonach Eagach ridge – not a place for casual exploration!

> There is little choice of route along this stretch, so you can saunter or race along as you wish, though in poor visibility this is no place to explore away from the path. Quite a few of the navvies working on the reservoir are known to have perished along this stretch as they lost their way in bad conditions.

Having crossed the tip of Sron a'Choire Odhair-bhig, the Way continues to cross Allt a'Choire Odhair-mhoir and presses on to come into sight of the huge black pipelines that traverse the hillsides from the reservoir. At one point the Way loops in a south-westerly direction to cross the Allt Choire Mhorair in a birch-wooded glen, by a bridge, before resuming its journey to Kinlochleven.

On the approach to Kinlochleven, as the path runs beside black water-pipes, it is deflected right, behind the aluminium works, to a bridge across the River Leven. Beyond the bridge it runs into the edge of a housing estate at Kinlochmore. A short way along the road, the Way leaves the road on the left for a constructed pathway through woodland, not far from the river, and rises on a pathway on the right just as it reaches the road bridge (B863) through Kinlochleven. A slanting track leads up to the road and an information panel.

Buchaille Etive Mor

Kinlochleven to Fort William

Distance:	22.5km (14 miles)
Ascent:	400m (1315 feet)

The remaining stage to the end of the Way begins with a steady rise from Kinlochleven to gain Lairig Mor, a fascinating and wholly unexpected glen that is the preserve only of pedestrians and estate workers, and concealed behind the high ridged summits of Mam na Gualainn and Beinn na Caillich. Beyond the glen the route swings northwards, leaving the military road near Blar a'Chaorainn to start its final rush to the embrace of Glen Nevis and journey's end. This is quite a long stage, with no refreshments and little shelter. Be sure, therefore, that you are fully prepared and provisioned before leaving the many facilities of Kinlochleven behind.

With parts of the township forever pitched in shade during the winter months and set so far from modern through-routes, it is not surprising that Kinlochleven has earned an unenviable reputation. W H Murray certainly was not enamoured of the place, describing it as 'The ugliest [township] on two thousand miles of Highland coast, this through an industry of high social value employing nearly a thousand men and women'. He does, however, relent a little as his view widens, commenting that 'Kinlochleven nestles at the foot of the Mamore Forest, a range of spiry mountains seen well from the high road of approach. The mountain scale is great enough to absorb the town into itself, so that … wood, loch, and mountain wholly dominate the scene, the town shrinking to merely wart-like dimension'.

Kinlochleven, which today very much thrives on the passage of Wayfarers, at the turn of the century was little more than two independent settlements, Kinlochmore and Kinlochbeg, until expansion came with the building there of the British Aluminium Company.

The growth of Kinlochleven reflected the growth of aluminium as a metal much demanded for modern technology, notably for the motor and aircraft industries.

Alas, the dramatic world-wide expansion of these markets marked the beginning of decline for Kinlochleven simply because much larger plants than that at Kinlochleven were able to benefit through the economies of scale. Their more powerful and aggressive economic infrastructure inevitably rendered smaller plants less efficient and more vulnerable to fluctuations in demand and price.

Kinlochleven is proud of a unique purity of its metal, but even this quality is no guarantee of long-term survival. Walkers treading the Way may find Kinlochleven's 'Aluminium Story' little more than a closed chapter in the social and economic history of the town. Tourism and the attentions of Wayfarers does much to help the local economy.

For many years the way northwards lay through Kinlochleven or by way of the Ballachulish ferry, which though regular was of limited capacity. Many were the times I queued at Ballachulish, calculating the wait, and deciding that it would be quicker to drive around the loch. In 1975 all that changed with the opening of the Ballachulish bridge.

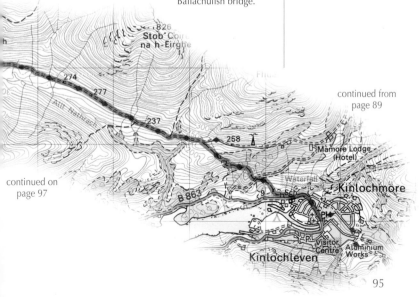

continued from page 89

continued on page 97

Mamore Lodge, now a hotel, perches high up on the flank of Am Bodach. It was formerly a shooting lodge used by King Edward VII, and it has for years provided a base for walkers venturing into the Mamores along the many deer stalking tracks and disused roads that criss-cross the mountainsides.

Resuming the journey, walk down the road, heading roughly north-west, out of the town, as far as a waymark and signpost on the right (Footpath to Glen Nevis by the Lairig). The Way continues by rising steadily as a stony track through birch scrub until, at a waymark, the path forks. Branch left here to cross a burn, and press on steeply through more scrub to reach a surfaced lane serving Mamore Lodge.

Cross the hotel access, and resume your upward plod through more woodland. After a while the path rises to a junction with a track that has risen from the valley road, and continues ascending in zigzags for some distance until, finally, clear of the woodland scrub, it rejoins the military road at a waymark. Turn left and begin a gradual descent.

Once the military road is reached, the walking becomes much easier and the onward route never in question, leaving you free to take in a superb panorama that embraces the Munros behind Ballachulish, and pinnacled sections of the Aonach Eagach, probably the finest continuous ridge walk on mainland Britain. The ridge then leads the eye to the Pap of Glencoe (Sgorr na Ciche), which effectively and neatly closes the view down Loch Leven to the west.

With plenty of opportunity to concentrate on your surroundings, the Way progresses steadily towards a high point beyond the Allt Nathrach, following which, it descends to the first of two deserted steadings, Tigh-na-sleubhaich. The second, a short distance further on, is Lairigmor, and both are evocative reminders of a distant, lonely and hard-won existence that few these days could countenance.

The track continues stonily past both buildings, traversing superb and remote hill country along the southern flank of the western Mamores. Finally, it rounds the southern flanks of Mullach nan Coirean and its south-western satellite, Meall a'Chaorainn, to run north-wards with the Allt na Lairige Moire. For most of the way through the glen the path is now descending, and passes the site of more old shielings before entering woodland. Cattle would be brought to these high mountain pastures

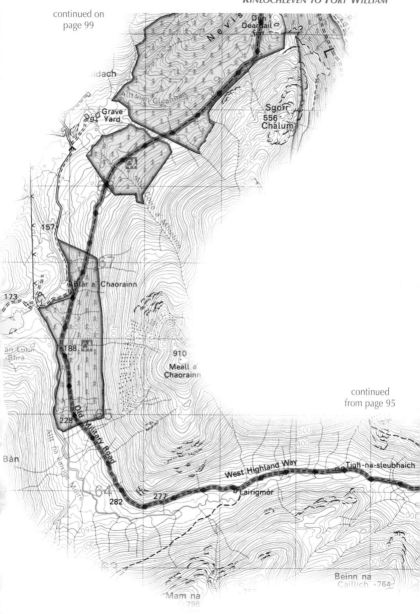

continued on
page 99

Nevis

Dùn
Deardail
fort

idach

Allt inn Gleannan

Grave
Yard

Sgorr
556
Chàlum

157

Blàr a' Chaorainn

173

188

910
Meall a
Chaorainn

continued
from page 95

228

Old Military Road

Bàn

West Highland Way

Tigh-na-sleubhaich

64

282   277

Lairigmór

Beinn na
Caillich · 764

Mam na
798

In a small glen to the side, as you exit the forest at an information panel, lies Lochan Lunn Da Bhra. In ancient times, Macbeth, King of the Scots from 1040 to 1057, is said to have resided on an island in the lochan, which was probably a crannog. The lochan is also supposed to have been inhabited by some kind of water bull, a mythical creature which emerged to kill grazing stock.

for grazing during the summer months, as they still are in parts of the French Alps and the Pyrenees.

Throughout the Lairig Mor section, the path is crossed by many burns issuing from the hillsides. Most are simple and easy to negotiate, others have footbridges, but in times of spate one or two could prove troublesome.

As you descend the track through the forest, and just before reaching Blar a'Chaorainn, you encounter a large cairn at the side of the track. In 1645, after the Battle of Inverlochy, MacDonalds from Montrose's army pursued a number of Argyll's defeated forces through this area, and the cairn is said to represent the spot where the MacDonalds gave up the chase.

On reaching the edge of the forest the Way finally abandons Caulfield's road close by the remains of a toll house.

The road has been your guide for some time, since Glen Falloch, so the romantic among you may be permitted to shed a tear, drink a toast, or otherwise mark the occasion of the parting as you see fit. Anyone feeling especially weary or running short of time, however, should

Glen Nevis

consider remaining with the road, not an unacceptable proposition, which provides a much easier stage into Fort William. Certainly you get a good view of Loch Linnhe and Fort William by pursuing this option, which is not available to the main route.

The final stage involves some rough and trying walking through extensive woodland before giving in gracefully and slipping down into Glen Nevis for the final stretch of road walking and increasing urbanisation to Bridge of Nevis.

The Way branches right from the old military road just beyond the information panel, rising on a track into

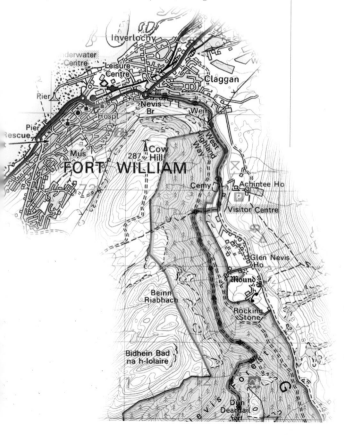

continued from page 97

99

Ben Nevis from Corpach

more forest, and shortly it leaves at a large step-stile over a deer fence, continuing as a stepped pathway before coming down to re-enter forest at another deer fence. Quickly, it runs down to cross an attractive burn by a footbridge, before passing on through more mature larch and pine.

> On the way, there is a view of Meall an t-Suidhe and Ben Nevis that could well represent another day's walking for the very fit. The Ben is not showing you its most attractive face from this angle, quite the opposite, but it never fails to impress with its sheer bulk and domination of all the surrounding countryside.

After a brief clearing the track continues through more forest to descend a constructed flight of steps to a footbridge over a burn beside a large boulder. Beyond that it presses on more or less horizontally for some time, before climbing steeply to the top edge of the forest where, at one final deer fence, the Way breaks out from the forest.

> A new path has been created beside the final fence to give access to Dun Deardail, a vitrified fort dating back to the Iron Age. It is not far to go to reach it, so if you have the time and interest, do so. The rubble walls of the fort were fused into a glassy mass by fire, which may have occurred accidentally or as a result of attack by raiders.
>
> Hill forts were quite common throughout Britain from about 500BC until the end of the first century, and ranged in size from fairly substantial constructions to small, simple structures that served as a form of defence against attack.

A stony path now steadily descends shortly to reach a main forest trail which shepherds you downwards into the glen. After some time, at a sharp bend, you meet a couple of waymarks. One identifies the most direct route to Glen Nevis Youth Hostel, for those bound for an overnight stay there. The other keeps left for a little while until it, too, meets a waymark that takes you off the forest trail and down an easy path to meet the glen road.

All that remains is for you to turn left and simply follow the road the remaining distance to the end of the West Highland Way at Bridge of Nevis.

> On the way, you will pass a large boulder by the road-side, the so-called Wishing Stone or Stone of Counsel (Clach Comhairle) to which various legends have been ascribed, including one which avows that at times the whole rock rotates and settles down again. Anyone encountering the stone while in its rotation (it only occurs on one night of the year – my money is on Hogmanay!) will get answers to any three questions put to the stone.

Well done! I hope you enjoyed the West Highland Way as much as I did.

APPENDICES

APPENDIX A: ACCOMMODATION GUIDE

CAMPING

To camp as you tramp along the West Highland Way, or indeed on any long-distance trail, rewards you with a close familiarity with nature and the environment, but places on you a responsibility to care for it – taking nothing but memories, leaving behind nothing but footprints.

Camping is certainly the most flexible way of getting about, but means considerably more weight to carry and the ability to cope in isolated situations and all weathers.

There are a few camp sites along the Way at:

Milngavie: Bankell Farm
Tel: 0141 956 1733
Email: info@bankellfarm.co.uk
Website: www.bankellfarm.co.uk

Wishing Well Coffee Shop Campsite
Gartness, Killearn
Open: 9am–5pm
Tel: 01360 551038 / 550062

Easter Drumquhassle
near Drymen
Tel: 01360 660893

Ardlui Hotel and Holiday Home Park
Tel: 01301 704243
Website: www.ardlui.co.uk

Inverarnan: Beinglas Farm
Tel: 01301 704281
Email: beinglas.campsite@virgin.net
Website: www.beinglascampsite.co.uk

Strathfillan, Tyndrum: Auchtertyre Farm
Tel: 01838 400251
Email: wigwam@au.sac.ac.uk

Kinlochleven:
Blackwater Hostel and Campsite
Tel: 01855 831253 / 402
Mobile: 07919 366116
Email: enquiries@blackwaterhostel.co.uk
Website: www.blackwaterhostel.co.uk

and Macdonald Hotel
and Lochside Campsite
Tel: 01855 831539
Email: enquiries@macdonaldhotel.co.uk
Website: www.macdonaldhotel.co.uk

Glen Nevis
Tel: 01397 702191
Email: holidays@glen-nevis.co.uk
Website: www.glen-nevis.co.uk

Note: Wild camping is not allowed on or around Conic Hill; on Forestry Commission land; along Loch Lomond and Glen Falloch from Rob Roy's Cave to Crianlarich; from Tyndrum to Inveroran; from Forest Lodge to Kinlochleven.

Elsewhere, if you are camping in the vicinity of dwellings, you should ask permission first.

WIGWAMS

These simple wooden structures provide the most basic accommodation in the form of a sleeping platform, but nothing else. They are found near farms or villages, which do offer facilities, and, being inexpensive, pre-booking would be a good idea during the summer months. You will find wigwams at:

Easter Drumquhassle Farm, Gartness Road, Drymen G63 0DN
Tel: 01360 660893

Beinglas Farm, Glen Falloch, Inverarnan G83 7DX
Tel: 01301 704281
for more information visit www.beinglascampsite.co.uk

Auchtertyre Farm, Strathfillan, Tyndrum, Crianlarich FK20 8RU
Tel: 01838 400251
for more information visit www.wigwamholidays.com/strathfillan

BUNKHOUSES AND PRIVATE HOSTELS

A few bunkhouses and private hostels exist along the Way, usually in association with a hotel or guest house offering a wider range of services. They often form part of a growing network of private hostels throughout Scotland. Along the Way you will find them at Bridge of Orchy, Kingshouse, Kinlochleven, Fort William, Tyndrum and Glen Nevis.

YOUTH HOSTELS

The Scottish Youth Hostels Association have three excellent hostels along the Way, plus one at the western end of Glencoe. You need to be a member, but can join at a hostel. They are all immensely popular, so advance booking is always a good idea during the main tourist periods.

Central reservations: 0870 1 55 32 55

Rowardennan By Drymen (GR359992), Glasgow G63 0AR
Hostel Tel: 0870 004 1148

Crianlarich (GR386250), Station Road, Crianlarich FK20 8QN
Hostel Tel: 0870 004 1112

Glencoe (GR118577), Ballachulish, Argyll PH49 4HX
Hostel Tel: 0870 004 1122

Glen Nevis (GR127716), Fort William, Inverness-shire PH33 6SY
Hostel Tel: 0870 004 1120

For details of other hostels near the Way, contact the Scottish Youth Hostels Association (see 'Appendix B: Useful Addresses')

ACCOMMODATION BOOKING SERVICES

A-M-S West Highland Way Services
13 Mosswater Wynd
Smithstone Gate   Tel: 01236 722664
Glasgow   Email: info@ams-scotland.com
G68 9JU   Website: www.ams-scotland.com

Easyways
Room 32, Haypark Business Centre
Marchmont Avenue
Polmont, Falkirk   Tel: 01324 714132
Stirlingshire   Email: info@easyways.com
FK2 0NZ   Website: www.easyways.com

PACK CARRYING SERVICES

A-M-S Rucksack Transfers
13 Mosswater Wynd
Smithstone Gate   Tel: 01236 722664
Glasgow   Email: info@ams-scotland.com
G68 9JU   Website: www.ams-scotland.com

Travel-Lite
The Iron Chef
5 Mugdock Road
Milngavie   Tel: 0141 956 7890
Glasgow   Email: info@travel-lite-uk.com
G628PD   Website: www.travel-lite-uk.com

HOTELS AND BED AND BREAKFAST

If you are planning to use a hotel or B&B for your overnight stays, it is always wise to book in advance, and during the key visitor period, essentially so. All the accommodation listed below is within a mile or so of the Way; any that is further invariably offers a pick-up service. The number of places offering accommodation services is growing all the time, so this list cannot ever be complete, but the author would welcome a note of any additional places (via the publisher) for inclusion in future editions of this guide. It is worth noting that you can pick up an annual accommodation list from Scottish Natural Heritage.

[Unless indicated the establishments are B&Bs, guest houses or hotels.]

Milngavie

Burnbrae Premier Lodge
Milngavie Road
Bearsden
G61 3TA
Tel: 0870 990 6532

Drumlin Guest House
93 Drumlin Drive
Milngavie
G62 6NF
Tel: 0141 956 1596

Mrs C Gardner
Barloch Guest House
82 Strathblane Road
Milngavie
G62 8DH
Tel: 0141 956 1432

High Craigton Farm
Stockiemuir Road
Milngavie
G62 7HA
Tel: 0141 956 1384

Kilmardinny Guest House
Milngavie Road
Bearsden
G61 3DH
Tel: 0141 943 1310
(Room only, no breakfast)

West Highland Gate
103 Main Street
Milngavie
G62 6JQ
Tel: 0870 197 7112
Email: westhighlandgate.milngavie@
whitbread.com

West View Guest House
1 Dougalston Gardens South
Milngavie
G62 6HS
Tel: 0141 956 3046
Email: bffmorag@aol.com

Drymen

Buchanan Arms Hotel
Main Street
Drymen
G63 0BQ
Tel: 01360 660588
Email: enquiries@buchananarms.co.uk
Website: www.buchananarms.co.uk

Mrs Betty Robb
Ceardach
Gartness Road
Drymen
G63 0BH
Tel: 01360 660596

Dorothy & John Reid
Croftburn B&B
Croftamie
Drymen
G63 0HA
Tel: 01360 660796
Email: enquiries@croftburn.co.uk
Website: www.croftburn.co.uk

Easter Balfunning Farm
Drymen
G63 0NF
Tel: 01360 440755

Easter Drumquhassle Farm
Gartness Road
Drymen
G63 0DN
Tel: 01360 660893
Email: juliamacx@aol.com

Elmbank
10 Stirling Road
Drymen
G63 0BN
Tel: 01360 661016
Website: www.elmbank-drymen.com

Mrs Yvonne Ford
Gateside Lodge
Gartness Road
By Drymen
G63 0DW
Tel: 01360 660215

Glenalva
Stirling Road
Drymen
G63 0AA
Tel: 01360 660491
Email: frasers@glenalva-drymen.co.uk
Website: www.glenalva-drymen.co.uk

The Hawthorns
1 Gartness Road
The Square
Drymen
G63 0BH
Tel: 01360 660916

Knopogue
Gateside
Gartness Road
Drymen
G63 0BH
Tel: 01360 660735

Lander B&B
17 Stirling Road
Drymen
G63 0BW
Tel: 01360 660273

Winnock Hotel
The Square
Drymen
G63 0BL
Tel: 01360 660245
Email: info@winnockhotel.com
Website: www.winnockhotel.co.uk

Milton of Buchanan

Dunleen
Milton of Buchanan
Drymen
G63 0JE
Tel: 01360 870274

Peter & Glennys Nichols
Mar Achlais Guest House
Milton of Buchanan
Drymen
G63 0JE
Tel: 01360 870300
Email: marachlais@dsl.pipex.com

Balmaha

Elizabeth Bates
Bay Cottage
Balmaha
G63 0JQ
Tel: 01360 870346

Oak Tree Inn
Balmaha
G63 0JQ
Tel: 01360 870357
Email: info@oak-tree-inn.co.uk
Website: www.oak-tree-inn.co.uk

Conic View Cottage
Balmaha Road
Balmaha
G63 0JQ
Tel: 01360 870297
Website: www.conicview.co.uk

Rowardennan

Anchorage Cottage
Rowardennan
G63 0AW
Tel: 01360 870394
Email: anchorage@tiscali.co.uk

Ben Lomond Cottage
Rowardennan
G63 0AR
Tel: 01360 870411

Corrie Doon
5 Forest Cottages
Rowardennan
G63 0AW
Tel: 01360 870320

Northwood Cottage
Sallochy
Rowardennan
G63 0AW
Tel: 01360 870351

Rowardennan Hotel
Rowardennan
By Drymen
G63 0AR
Tel: 01360 870273
Email: stay@rowardennanhotel.co.uk
Website: www.rowardennanhotel.co.uk

Inversnaid, Ardlui and Inverarnan

Inversnaid Lodge
Inversnaid
By Aberfoyle
Stirling
FK8 3TU
Tel: 01877 386254

Ardlui Hotel
Loch Lomond
Argyle
G83 7EB
Tel: 01301 704243 / 269
Email: info@ardlui.co.uk
Website: www.ardluihotel.com

Beinglas Farm
Inverarnan
Ardlui
By Arrochar
G83 7DX
Tel: 01301 704281
Email: beinglas.campsite@virgin.net
Website: www.beinglascampsite.co.uk

Inverarnan Drovers
By Ardlui
G83 7DX
Tel: 01301 704234
Email: info@theinnonlochlomond.com
Website: www.thedroversinn.co.uk

Rose Cottage
Inverarnan
G83 7DX
Tel: 01301 704255

Crianlarich

Ben More Lodge Hotel
Crianlarich
FK20 8QS
Tel: 01838 300210
Email: info@ben-more.co.uk
Website: www.ben-more.co.uk

Craigbank Guest House
Crianlarich
FK20 8QS
Tel: 01838 300279

Glenardran Guest House
Crianlarich
FK20 8QS
Tel: 01838 300236

Suie Lodge Hotel
Glendochart
Crianlarich
FK20 8QT
Tel: 01567 820417
Email: info@suielodge.co.uk
Website: www.suielodge.co.uk

Tigh na Struith
Crianlarich
FK20 8RU
Tel: 01838 300235

Strathfillan and Tyndrum

Auchtertyre Farm
Tyndrum
FK20 8RU
Tel: 01838 400251

By the Way
Lower Station Road
Tyndrum
FK20 8RY
Tel: 01838 400333

Dalkell
Tyndrum
FK20 8RZ
Tel: 01838 400285
Email: dalkell@btopenworld.com
Website: www.dalkell.com

Ewich House
Strathfillan
Crianlarich
FK20 8RU
Tel: 01838 300300
Email: enquiries@ewich.co.uk
Website: www.ewich.co.uk

Glengarry Guest House
Tyndrum
FK20 8RY
Tel: 01838 400224
Email: enquiries@glengarryhouse.co.uk
Website: www.glengarryhouse.co.uk

Invervey Hotel
Tyndrum
FK20 8RY
Tel: 01838 400219
Email: info@inverveyhotel.co.uk
Website: www.inverveyhotel.co.uk

Bridge of Orchy

Glen Orchy Farm
Bridge of Orchy
PA33 1BD
Tel: 01838 200 399 / 200 450
Email: theoldhouse@glen-orchy.co.uk
Website: www.glen-orchy.co.uk

Bridge of Orchy Hotel
Bridge of Orchy
PA36 4AD
Tel: 01838 400208
Email: info@bridgeoforchy.co.uk
Website: www.bridgeoforchy.co.uk

Inveroran

Inveroran Hotel
Bridge of Orchy
PA36 4AQ
Tel: 01838 400220
Email: booking@inveroran.com

Kingshouse

King's House Hotel
Kingshouse
Glencoe
PA39 4HY
Tel: 01855 851259
Website: www.kingy.com

Kinlochleven

Ardbeg
Wades Road,
Kinlochleven
Tel: 01855 831224

Edencoille Guest House
Garbhein Road
Kinlochleven
PH40 4SE
Tel: 01855 831358

Blackwater Hostel
Kinlochleven
Argyll
PH50 4RS
Tel: 01855 831253 / 402
Mobile: 07919 366116
Email: enquiries@blackwaterhostel.co.uk
Website: www.blackwaterhostel.co.uk

Failte
6 Lovat Road
Kinlochleven
PH50 4RQ
Tel: 01855 831394

Hermon
Rob Roy Road
Kinlochleven
PH40 4RA
Tel: 01855 831383

MacDonald Hotel
Fort William Road
Kinlochleven
PH40 4QL
Tel: 01855 831539
enquiries@macdonaldhotel.co.uk
Website: www.macdonaldhotel.co.uk

Mr Paul Bush
Mamore Lodge Hotel
Kinlochleven
PH50 4QN
Tel: 01855 831213
Website: www.mamorelodge.co.uk

Quiraing
43 Lovat Road
Kinlochleven
PH40 4RQ
Tel: 01855 831580

Tailrace Inn
Riverside Road
Kinlochleven
PH40 4QH
Tel: 01855 831777
Email: tailrace@btconnect.com
Website: www.tailraceinn.co.uk

Tigh-na-Cheo Guest House
Garbhein Road
Kinlochleven
PH50 4SE
Tel: 01855 831434
Email: reception@tigh-na-cheo.co.uk
Website: www.tigh-na-cheo.co.uk

West Highland Lodge (Bunkhouse)
Kinlochleven
PH40 4RT
Tel: 01855 831471

Fort William

Achintee Farm Guest House
Glen Nevis
Fort William
PH33 6TE
Tel: 01397 702240
Email: hostel@achinteefarm.com
Website: www.achinteefarm.com

Alexandra Milton Hotel
The Parade
Fort William
PH33 6AZ
Tel: 01397 702241

Ardblair
Fassifern Road
Fort William
PH33 6LJ
Tel: 01397 705832
Email: stay@ardblairfortwilliam.co.uk
Website: www.ardblairfortwilliam.co.uk

Ashburn House
7 Achintore Road
Fort William
PH33 6RQ
Tel: 01397 706000
Email: stay@ashburnhouse.co.uk
Website: www.ashburnhouse.co.uk

Mrs C A Smith
Ben View Guest House
Belford Road
Fort William
PH33 6ER
Tel: 01397 702966
Website:
www.benviewguesthouse.co.uk

Crochaorich
Achintee Road
Fort William
Tel: 01397 704669

Mr Alan Kimber
Calluna (Bunkhouse)
Heathercroft
Fort William
PH33 6RE
Tel: 01397 700451

Stuart & Mandy McLean
Distillery House
Nevis Bridge
North Road
Fort William
Tel: 01397 700103

Dunollie
9 Ardnevis Road
Fort William
Tel: 01397 702502

Glenfer
Glen Nevis
Fort William
PH33 6ST
Tel: 01397 705848

Glenlochy Guest House
Nevis Bridge
Fort William
PH33 6PF
Tel: 01397 702909
Email: glenlochy1@aol.com
Website:
www.glenlochyguesthouse.co.uk

Lochview Guest House
Heathercroft Road
Fort William
PH33 6RE
Tel: 01397 703149
Email: info@lochview.co.uk
Website: www.lochview.co.uk

Mrs J MacLeod
25 Alma Road
Fort William
PH33 6HD
Tel: 01397 703735

Mrs Ann Munro
62 Alma Road
Fort William
PH33 6H0
Tel: 01397 701685

Nevis Bank Hotel
Belford Road
Fort William
PH33 6BY
Tel: 01397 705721
Email: info@nevisbankhotel.co.uk
Website: www.nevisbankhotel.co.uk

Ian MacPherson
Rhu Mhor Guest House
Alma Road
Fort William
PH33 6BP
Tel: 01397 702213
Website: www.rhumhor.co.uk

WALKERS WELCOME SCHEME

Quite a number of establishments listed above are part of the 'Walkers Welcome Scheme'. Wherever you see the sign for the scheme, walkers are ensured of a warm welcome. In return, walkers are asked to consider the needs of the proprietors and their other guests, and to bear in mind that many establishments along the Way cater for visitors whose needs are different from those of walkers. The Walkers Welcome Scheme should mean that courteous walkers always receive a courteous welcome.

Of course, it does not follow that establishments not currently operating as part of the scheme will extend anything less than traditional Highland hospitality.

APPENDIX B: USEFUL ADDRESSES

TOURIST BOARDS

All enquiries for tourist information in Scotland are now handled through the main Visit Scotland centre in Edinburgh.

Visit Scotland
23 Ravelston Terrace, Edinburgh EH4 3TP
Tel: 0131 332 2433
Email: info@visitscotland.com
Website: www.visitscotland.com

Glasgow City Marketing Bureau
11 George Square, Glasgow G2 1DY
Tel: 0141 566 0800
Email: info@seeglasgow.com
Website: www.seeglasgow.com
Tourist information enquiries should also be referred to Visit Scotland Glasgow on Tel: 0141 204 4400

Argyll, the Isles, Loch Lomond, Stirling and the Trossachs
Old Town Jail, St. John Street, Stirling FK8 1EA
Website: www.visitscottishheartlands.com

Highlands of Scotland
Peffery House, Strathpeffer, Inverness IV14 9IIA
Tel: 01997 421160
Email: info@visitscotland.com
Website: www.visithighlands.com

TOURIST INFORMATION CENTRES

Balloch
Old Station Building, Balloch Road, Balloch, G83 8LQ
Open: Apr–Oct.
Tel: 08707 200 607
Email: info@balloch.visitscotland.com

Balloch: National Park Gateway Centre

Loch Lomond Shores, Balloch G83 8LQ
Open: Apr–Oct
Tel: 08707 200 631
Email: info@lochlomond.visitscotland.com

Drymen

Drymen Library, The Square, Drymen, G63 0BD
Open: May–Sept
Tel: 08707 200 611
Email: info@drymen.visitscotland.com

Tyndrum

Main Street, Tyndrum, Perthshire FK20 8RY
Tel: 08707 200 626
Fmail: info@tyndrum.visitscotland.com

Fort William

Cameron Square, Fort William, PH33 6AJ
Tel: 01397 703781
Email: info@fortwilliam.visitscotland.com

ORGANISATIONS

Loch Lomond and the Trossachs National Park

The Old Station, Balloch Road, Balloch, G83 8BF
Tel. 01389 722600
Email: info@lochlomond-trossachs.org
Website: www.lochlomond-trossachs.org

Ordnance Survey

Romsey Road, Maybush, Southampton SO16 4GU
Tel: 08456 05 05 05
Email: customerservices@ordnancesurvey.co.uk
Website: www.ordnancesurvey.co.uk

The Mountaineering Council of Scotland
The Old Granary, West Mill Street, Perth PH1 5QP
Tel: 01738 493942
Email: info@mountaineering-scotland.org.uk
Website: www.mountaineering-scotland.org.uk

The National Trust for Scotland
Wemyss House, 28 Charlotte Square, Edinburgh EH2 4ET
Tel: 0131 243 9300
Email: information@nts.org.uk
Website: www.nts.org.uk

Scottish Natural Heritage
Great Glen House, Leachkin Road, Inverness IV3 8NW
Tel: 01463 725000
Email: enquiries@snh.gov.uk
Website: www.snh.org.uk

Scottish Rights of Way and Access Society
24 Annandale Street, Edinburgh EH7 4AN
Tel: 0131 558 1222
Email: info@scotways.com
Website: www.scotways.com

Scottish Youth Hostels Association
7 Glebe Crescent, Stirling FK8 2JA
Website: www.syha.org.uk

General enquiries
Tel: 01786 891 400
Email: info@syha.org.uk

For reservations
Tel 0870 1 55 32 55
Email: reservations@syha.org.uk

APPENDIX C:

ESSENTIAL AND SUPPLEMENTARY READING

J H B Bell, *Bell's Scottish Climbs* (Gollancz, 1988)

George Rowntree Harvey, *A Book of Scotland* (A and C Black, 1949; reprint, 1953)

G F Maine (ed.), *A Book of Scotland* (Collins, 1950 and 1972)

Mary B Bruce, *The Buchanans: Some Historical Notes* (Stirling District Libraries, 1995)

W H Murray, *The Companion Guide to the West Highlands of Scotland*, 7th ed. (Collins, 1977)

A R B Haldane, *The Drove Roads of Scotland* (House of Lochar, 1995)

John Prebble, *Glencoe* (Penguin Books, 1978)

Maurice Lindsay, *The Lowlands of Scotland: Glasgow and the North* (Robert Hale, 1979)

William Taylor, *The Military Roads in Scotland* (House of Lochar, 1996)

W H Murray, *Mountaineering in Scotland and Undiscovered Scotland* (Diadem, 1979)

Brian Paul Hindle, *Roads, Tracks and their Interpretation* (Batsford, 1993)

Sir Walter Scott, *Rob Roy* (Dent, Everyman's Library No. 142, 1966)

Nigel Tranter, *The Story of Scotland* (Lochar Publishing, 1987)

Donald Bennet, *The Southern Highlands* (Scottish Mountaineering Trust, 1972)

NOTES

NOTES

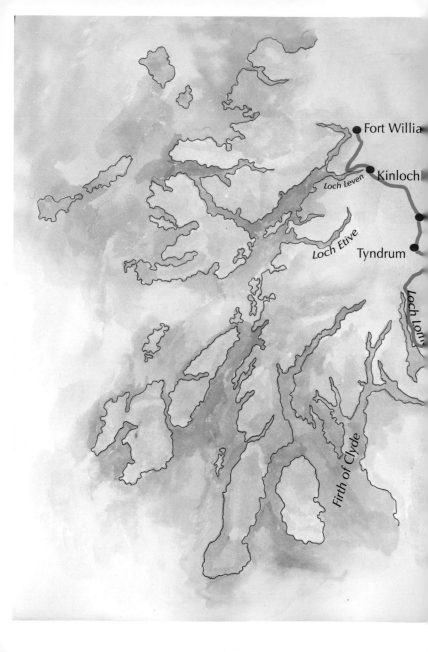

n

dge of Orchy

Crianlarich

Aberfoyle

Dundee

Drymen

Milngavie

Glasgow

Edinburgh

The West Highland Way

LISTING OF CICERONE GUIDES

Walking in the Harz Mountains
Walking in the Salzkammergut
Walking the River Rhine Trail

HIMALAYA
Annapurna: A Trekker's Guide
Bhutan
Everest: A Trekker's Guide
Garhwal and Kumaon: A
Trekker's and Visitor's Guide
Kangchenjunga: A Trekker's
Guide
Langtang with Gosainkund and
Helambu: A Trekker's Guide
Manaslu: A Trekker's Guide
The Mount Kailash Trek

IRELAND
Irish Coastal Walks
The Irish Coast to Coast Walk
The Mountains of Ireland

ITALY
Central Apennines of Italy
Gran Paradiso
Italian Rock
Italy's Sibillini National Park
Shorter Walks in the Dolomites
Through the Italian Alps
Trekking in the Apennines
Treks in the Dolomites
Via Ferratas of the Italian
Dolomites
Vols 1 & 2
Walking in Sicily
Walking in the Central Italian
Alps
Walking in the Dolomites
Walking in Tuscany
Walking on the Amalfi Coast

MEDITERRANEAN
Jordan – Walks, Treks, Caves,
Climbs and Canyons
The Ala Dag
The High Mountains of Crete
The Mountains of Greece
Treks and Climbs in Wadi Rum,
Jordan
Walking in Malta
Western Crete

NORTH AMERICA
British Columbia
The Grand Canyon

The John Muir Trail
The Pacific Crest Trail

SOUTH AMERICA
Aconcagua and the Southern
Andes
Torres del Paine

SCANDINAVIA
Trekking in Greenland
Walking in Norway

SLOVENIA, CROATIA AND
MONTENEGRO

The Julian Alps of Slovenia
The Mountains of Montenegro
Trekking in Slovenia
Walking in Croatia

SPAIN AND PORTUGAL
Costa Blanca Walks
1 West
2 East
Mountain Walking in Southern
Catalunya
The Mountains of Central Spain
Trekking through Mallorca
Via de la Plata
Walking in Madeira
Walking in Mallorca
Walking in the Algarve
Walking in the Canary Islands
2 East
Walking in the Cordillera
Cantabrica
Walking in the Sierra Nevada
Walking on La Gomera and
El Hierro
Walking on La Palma
Walking the GR7 in Andalucia
Walks and Climbs in the Picos
de Europa

SWITZERLAND
Alpine Pass Route
Central Switzerland
The Bernese Alps
Tour of the Jungfrau Region
Walking in the Valais
Walking in Ticino
Walks in the Engadine

TECHNIQUES
Indoor Climbing
Map and Compass

Mountain Weather
Moveable Feasts
Outdoor Photography
Rock Climbing
Snow and Ice Techniques
Sport Climbing
The Book of the Bivvy
The Hillwalker's Guide to
Mountaineering
The Hillwalker's Manual

MINI GUIDES
Avalanche!
Navigating with a GPS
Navigation
Pocket First Aid and Wilderness
Medicine
Snow

For full and up-to-date
information on our ever-
expanding list of guides,
visit our website:
www.cicerone.co.uk.

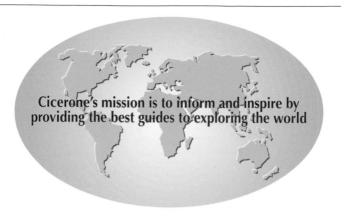

Cicerone's mission is to inform and inspire by providing the best guides to exploring the world

Since its foundation 40 years ago, Cicerone has specialised in publishing guidebooks and has built a reputation for quality and reliability. It now publishes nearly 300 guides to the major destinations for outdoor enthusiasts, including Europe, UK and the rest of the world.

Written by leading and committed specialists, Cicerone guides are recognised as the most authoritative. They are full of information, maps and illustrations so that the user can plan and complete a successful and safe trip or expedition – be it a long face climb, a walk over Lakeland fells, an alpine cycling tour, a Himalayan trek or a ramble in the countryside.

With a thorough introduction to assist planning, clear diagrams, maps and colour photographs to illustrate the terrain and route, and accurate and detailed text, Cicerone guides are designed for ease of use and access to the information.

If the facts on the ground change, or there is any aspect of a guide that you think we can improve, we are always delighted to hear from you.

Cicerone Press
2 Police Square Milnthorpe Cumbria LA7 7PY
Tel: 015395 62069 Fax: 015395 63417
info@cicerone.co.uk www.cicerone.co.uk

CICERONE